A Reinhold Niebuhr Reader

A REINHOLD NIEBUHR READER

Selected Essays, Articles, and Book Reviews

Compiled and edited by

Charles C. Brown

Trinity Press International Philadelphia

First Edition 1992

Trinity Press International
3725 Chestnut Street
Philadelphia, PA 19104

Cover Design by Jim Gerhard
Cover Photo by Fabian Bachrach

Library of Congress Cataloging-in-Publication Data

Niebuhr, Reinhold, 1892–1971.
[Selections. 1992]
A Reinhold Niebuhr reader : selected essays, articles, and book reviews / compiled and edited by Charles C. Brown.
p. cm.
ISBN 1563380439 (pbk.) :
1. Theology—20th century. 2. Church and social problems. I. Brown, Charles C. (Charles Calvin), 1938– . II. Title.
BR85.N6242 1992
230—dc20 92-28345
CIP

Printed in the United States of America.

92 93 94 95 96 97 6 5 4 3 2 1

Contents

Acknowledgments

The publisher gratefully thanks the following for permission to reprint essays, articles, and reviews in this volume.

Fortune for "A Faith for History's Greatest Crisis." Reprinted by permission from *Fortune* magazine; © 1942 Time Inc. All rights reserved.

Yale University Press for "The Two Sources of Western Culture" in *The Christian Idea of Education*, edited by Edmund Fuller. Reprinted by permission of Yale University Press, © 1957.

Commentary for "Will Civilization Survive Technics?" Reprinted from *Commentary*, December 1945, by permission; all rights reserved.

Christianity and Crisis for "Christian Faith and Political Controversy," "The Christian Faith and the World Crisis," "The Death of the President," "Soberness in Victory," "American Power and European Health," "Will We Resist Injustice?" "Winston Churchill and Great Britain," "Coexistence under a Nuclear Stalemate," "The Mounting Racial Crisis," "John Fitzgerald Kennedy, 1917–1963," "Adlai Stevenson: 1900–1965," and "The Death of a Martyr." All reprinted with permission. Copyright © respectively 1952, 1941, 1945, 1945, 1947, 1953, 1955, 1959, 1963, 1963, 1965, 1945.

The Nation for "Halfway to What?" and reviews of Benedetto Croce's *History as the Story of Liberty*, Jacob Burckhardt's *Force and Freedom: Reflections on History*, Friedrich Hayek's *The Road to Serfdom*, Denis de Rougemont's *The Devil's Share*, Carl Becker's *Freedom and Responsibility in the American Way of Life*, Perry Miller's *Jonathan Edwards*, and *The God That Failed* by Arthur Koestler

Introduction

Theologian, social philosopher, journalist, and educator, Reinhold Niebuhr was born in Missouri in 1892, grew up in the parsonage of an Illinois prairie town, and graduated from what is now Elmhurst College (1910), Eden Theological Seminary (1913), and Yale University (B.D., 1914; M.A., 1915). After thirteen years as a pastor in Detroit, he taught Christian ethics at Union Theological Seminary from 1928 to 1960. Renowned for his Gifford Lectures, published as *The Nature and Destiny of Man* (1941–43), Niebuhr led a recovery in American Protestantism of its biblical and theological heritage in creative relationship to modern culture. In other books—among them *The Children of Light and the Children of Darkness* (1944), *The Irony of American History* (1952), and *The Self and the Dramas of History* (1955)—and in essays and articles in a variety of religious and secular journals, he further developed theological themes and set forth a pragmatic Christian realism as a basis for democratic politics and international relations.

Niebuhr was the founding editor of *Christianity and Crisis*, a biweekly that from 1941 onward carried his commentary on current events, and also of *Christianity and Society*, a small quarterly begun earlier and continuing to 1956. Once a socialist and a pacifist, he became an early and staunch supporter of the war against Nazi tyranny, and came to accept the legacy of Franklin Roosevelt in American domestic policy. A founder of Americans for Democratic Action, he backed containment of Soviet power in postwar Europe but advocated restraint in the use of American power as the Cold War spread to Asia and elsewhere. He gave timely support to the cause of a national homeland for the Jews and to the movement for belated justice to America's black minority. An avid reader as well as social activist, Niebuhr reviewed perceptively many important books over the years, ranging from Charles Norris Cochrane's *Christianity and Classical Culture* and a translation of Søren Kierkegaard's *Concluding Unscientific Postscript* to Gunnar Myrdal's *An American Dilemma* and James MacGregor Burns's *Roosevelt: The Lion and the Fox*. Receiving twenty-one honorary doctorates and elected to the American Academy of Arts and Letters in 1958, Reinhold Niebuhr resided during his last years in Stockbridge, Massachusetts, where he died in 1971.

This anthology is organized into five parts. The first consists of two memorable essays, a short piece on theology, and fragments from other theological writings. The second brings together three notable essays and various fragments on social philosophy. The third is a selection of articles on salient events and issues of the American and international scenes from the 1940s through the 1960s. The fourth is a treasure-trove of book reviews that appeared during the same period. The fifth consists of a few miscellaneous pieces and closes with a prayer.

The volume is organized in this manner even though theology and social philosophy are mingled in Niebuhr's works, and both suffuse his journalism. All of his writings here selected have been reprinted in full, except for several pieces in Part III that have been reduced, with ellipses showing where ephemeral or marginal passages are omitted. Where helpful, the editor has supplied introductory notes on context. The entire selection, drawn from Niebuhr's abundant shorter writings, is representative of his mature thought. All but two pieces are reprinted in this volume for the first time.

No selection of Reinhold Niebuhr's published writings can present his work in its fullness, but anthologies do make some of it conveniently available. Readers of this anthology will also want to consult nine other such volumes, each distinctive in scope and emphasis: *Love and Justice* (1957) and *Essays in Applied Christianity* (1959), edited by D. B. Robertson; *The World Crisis and American Responsibility* (1958), edited by Ernest W. Lefever; *Reinhold Niebuhr on Politics* (1960), edited by Harry R. Davis and Robert C. Good; *Faith and Politics* (1968), edited by Ronald H. Stone; *Justice and Mercy* (1974), edited by Ursula M. Niebuhr; *Young Reinhold Niebuhr* (1977), edited by William G. Chrystal; *The Essential Reinhold Niebuhr* (1986), edited by Robert McAfee Brown; and *Reinhold Niebuhr: Theologian of Public Life* (1989), edited by Larry Rasmussen.

Publication of this anthology, in the centennial year of Reinhold Niebuhr's birth, has been made possible by a generous grant from the Lynde and Harry Bradley Foundation. John C. Bennett, Nathan A. Scott, Jr., Roger L. Shinn, and Carl Hermann Voss—authorities on Niebuhr—and Alan R. Havig of Stephens College and Harold W. Rast of Trinity Press International assisted in selecting pieces for it.

Charles C. Brown
Columbia, Missouri
April 1992

PART I
THEOLOGY

A Faith for History's Greatest Crisis

[*Fortune,* Vol. 26 (July 1942), pp. 99–100, 122, 125–26, 128, 131.] While preparing the second volume of his Gifford Lectures for publication during World War II, Niebuhr wrote this essay setting forth a Christian perspective on history.

IN our own Western history the crisis in which we stand is the third in a series. The first was the fall of the Roman Empire. The second was the decay of feudalism and the rise of our own bourgeois democratic society. A brief survey of what occurred in these crises may illumine our own situation.

The Roman Empire fell after Christianity had been made the official religion of the empire; but Christianity lost something of its profundity in the process of its domestication in the empire. The prestige of Rome had been so great, the Pax Romana had become one of the "eternal verities" to such a degree, that men were threatened with despair when they saw this great system of "law and order" crumbling before their eyes. Furthermore, they felt that Christianity had lost its meaning, because they assumed that Christian truth had validated itself by arresting the decay of Roman civilization and that its final inability to stop the decay had invalidated it.

This sense of despair and confusion prompted the greatest philosopher of Christian history, Augustine, to write one of the most important books of our spiritual history: *The City of God.* In it he maintained that decay of Rome was not the end of all things, and certainly not a cause for despair. On the contrary he affirmed that the Christian religion contained an interpretation of life and history that made it possible to anticipate and to discount the periodic catastrophes of history. Every empire, every "city of this world," he declared, would have to break down ultimately because its "peace was based on strife." Which is to say that such social peace as is achieved in any civilization rests upon a precarious equilibrium of social forces. This equilibrium may degenerate into anarchy if there is no strong organizing center in it. And it may degenerate into tyranny if the organizing center destroys the vitality of the parts.

The new medieval society was, on the whole, built upon Christian presuppositions as defined by St. Augustine. But as medieval civilization finally integrated and organized the vast political and ethnic vitalities of Europe and achieved the social peace and equilibrium of the "golden" thirteenth century, it subtly compounded the complacency of a stable society with the profounder insights of Augustine. Augustine's conception of the tentativity of all historic achievements was lost. Medieval Christianity tended to define the characteristic social relations of a feudal-agrarian society as absolute and final. The invariable mistake of all cultures is that they tend to forget the relative character of such social justice and social peace as are achieved in a given civilization. And the greatest illusion of all historic cultures is that they mistake the precarious stability of their civilization for the final peace. They always fail to heed the warning: "If any man stand let him take heed lest he fall."

At the precise moment when medieval society celebrated its arrangements as essentially final, it proved that it was unable to absorb a new factor into its life and law. That new factor was expanding commerce. The vital agent of that new factor was the businessman. The businessman found himself excluded from the political and economic organization of feudal society. By a series of evolutionary and revolutionary processes, including the Cromwellian revolution in England, the revolution in France, and our own American revolution, the businessman finally established a new society, capitalistic in economic form and, broadly speaking, democratic in political form.

It seems to me to be futile to attempt the solution of our contemporary problems by counseling a simple return to the "medieval synthesis" and the medieval unity of culture and civilization. I admit that it was more profoundly conceived than some of our modern substitutes. But the point is that it was not able to incorporate the new factor of world commerce, the rising nation and the rising business classes, into its political and economic equilibriums. These new factors destroyed its stability. And one reason, at least, why it could not adjust itself to the new was that a religious culture, which ideally should have transcended the particular perspectives of feudalism, did in fact give religious, which means absolute, sanctity to the relative forms of justice and injustice that characterized an agrarian society of landlords and serfs. In consequence, the bourgeois rebels against the feudal society expressed themselves in terms of either a secular or a Protestant culture.

The civilization that we are now defending against the attack of a synthetic barbarism (even while we are conscious of the fact that only internal weaknesses could have made that attack possible and allowed it to come so close to a triumph over us) is one that has developed largely under the leadership of the bourgeois classes. It has been supplanting feudalism, beginning with the fourteenth century. It rose to its greatest heights in the nineteenth and the early part of the twentieth century. And it finds itself in one of the deepest crises of world history in our own generation.

Every great crisis in world history represents a breakdown both in the organization of civilization and in the life of a culture. It is a spiritual as well as a political and economic crisis. The two aspects of life may be distinguished, even though the distinction is slightly arbitrary, by the words "civilization" and "culture." Civilization is the body of a culture. Culture is the spirit of a civilization. Civilization means the political, economic, and social arrangements and mechanisms by which the life of men is ordered. Culture means the philosophical, esthetic, and religious ideas and presuppositions that inform the political organization and that in turn emerge from it.

Ideally an adequate culture would not be involved in the breakdown of a civilization. For an adequate culture would be an interpretation of the meaning of life and history, which would comprehend the periodic breakdowns of civilization as inevitable and would seek to appropriate the lessons to be learned from those breakdowns for the building of a better civilization. Actually this never quite happens for the reason that every culture tends to appropriate certain ideas and conceptions, which are the characteristic products and illusions of its own civilization, into its system of "eternal truths" and to imagine that life would be meaningless without them. It thus brings life fairly close to meaninglessness because the ideas that it regards as eternal are actually being destroyed in the crisis. Furthermore, this spiritual confusion tends to accentuate the political and social crisis; for in every great crisis confusion is worse confounded by the insistence of some that the very illusions that the crisis is challenging and destroying belong to the eternal verities, which cannot be destroyed.

The problem in every great historical crisis is therefore to find a philosophy of life sufficiently profound to be able to transcend both the political and moral confusion and to give a vantage point from which the errors, which brought it on, can be corrected.

From the standpoint of "civilization" rather than "culture," our own crisis is more complicated than that of either the Roman or the feudal decline. Like Rome, we are subject to external attack. But the external foe is not a "natural" but a "synthetic" barbarian. His barbarism has been generated out of the decay of our own unanswered problems. The decay within our own household is due not so much to the introduction of a new factor in the equilibrium of society as to the extension of the same factor that disturbed the Middle Ages. A commercial society has grown into an industrial one; and the industrial society has made use of technical instruments of communication and production of ever-increasing power. Technics have altered every aspect of our existence. Their incredibly rapid extension has disturbed every established social equilibrium. In the international field they have created a potential world community through the economic interdependence of the nations and through the increased proximity fashioned by rapid means of communication. But a potential world community that lacks political instruments for the regulation of its economic interdependence, the arbitration of its various conflicts, and the mitigation of its various frictions is bound, in fact, to become a state of international anarchy. The false answer to the problem of this anarchy is the Nazi tyrannical unification of the world. The instruments of a technical civilization increased the anarchy of our world, made the tyrannical alternative to anarchy more cruel in its methods, and enhanced the possibility of success for its ambitions of world dominion.

Furthermore, the uncontrolled potencies of a technical society have also brought confusion into our domestic life. The units of industrial production have been consistently enlarged, the old checks and balances of competitive enterprise have been imperiled or become atrophied, economic power has become more and more centralized, and the fabulous productivity of the modern machine has created crises and unemployment rather than security and abundance. Eighteenth-century dreams of a simple automatic harmony of all economic forces, if only irrelevant political restraints were removed from the economic process, have been cruelly disappointed.

It is not my province or purpose to analyze the political and economic maladjustments of contemporary civilization. I wish rather to call attention to the fact that *modern culture has no perspective from which it can view this confusion and plan a better world;* for all our cultural perspectives are themselves colored by the civilization that is involved. If, for instance, the optimistic assumption underlies a whole culture that the extension of technics inevitably makes for the advancement of the good life, such a culture can do little to save men from confusion and despair if the extension of technics actually aggravates domestic and foreign conflict at a particular juncture of history.

The fact is that the tragic realities in which Western civilization is involved are really striking refutations of our characteristic credos. It is particularly significant that millions of rational and "idealistic" people refused to take the monstrous perils of totalitarianism seriously because, according to their interpretation of history, no great peril could arise in a mature period of civilization. Monsters belonged by definition in the dawn of human history. Highly developed civilization had presumably domesticated all their beasts of prey. If, nevertheless, the monster seemed to be real, it was assumed that he was no more than a hungry beast of prey. If he were fed he would subside. So these good people suggested new trade agreements for the monster. The mania and the fury of the monster were interpreted as merely the hunger of a have-not nation. Or perhaps his lust could be satisfied by territory. Thus the sacrifice of Czechoslovakia was intended to bring "peace in our time." When all these devices failed, we talked about a "reversion to barbarism"; which means that we could imagine evil in history only as a return to a primitive past. We could not imagine that a mature civilization would produce in its decay, not the evils of nature or of primitive society, but terrible evils that are relevant to, and possible only in, maturity. We did not understand the difference between nature and history. In nature, beasts of prey lie down to go to sleep when their maws are crammed. In human history, no hunger is ever perfectly satisfied and grows by what it feeds on. Just as the desires of man are infinite so also are the possibilities for good and evil in history. But the possibilities for evil keep abreast of the possibilities for good. The delicate balances of a mature mind are more easily subject to disarrangement (insanity) than the simple psychic processes of a child; and a complex technical society can fall into more utter confusion than a simple agrarian economy. The cruelty of the Nazis is no more like "barbarism" than insanity is childishness. The persistent inclination of modern culture to minimize the monstrous evils against which we must contend, and to interpret them as reversions to nature or to a primitive past, reveals a false estimate of human history and a false confidence in its securities. The conflicts and catastrophes of our era have been the more terrible because we had no philosophy by which we could anticipate them, or understand them when they were upon us.

Our modern era, which followed the dissolution of the medieval culture and the feudal civilization, was ushered in by two great movements, the Renaissance and the Reformation. We must understand the relation between these two movements to comprehend the shallowness of contemporary culture and its incapacity for profound historical analysis. Reformation and Renaissance are frequently interpreted as closely allied movements by which the freedom and individualism of modern civilization were established. Whatever the affinities between them, they were actually diametrically opposed to each other in their main emphases. The Reformation regarded the medieval Catholic interpretation of life and history as too optimistic. Human history, according to the Reformation, never achieves such perfection, either individually or collectively, as the medieval era pretended to have achieved. The Reformation did not believe that there could ever be "Christian" societies, or governments, or economic arrangements in the exact ethical definition of the term. A civilization could be Christian only in the sense that it had a faith that would help it to understand, and contritely to admit, the inevitable egoistic and "sinful" corruption by which all human enterprises, including the church and religious institutions, were tainted.

The Renaissance criticized the Catholic ages from the very opposite point of view. It regarded the Christian interpretation of life as too pessimistic. It believed that the human mind had been fettered by religious authority and corrupted by religious superstition. It had great confidence that the "emancipated" mind would disclose the secrets of nature; penetrate into all the ultimate mysteries of life; exploit the buried treasures of the natural world and make them available for man; explore the complexities of human society and eliminate the social maladjustments that ignorance had perpetuated; finally turn its attention to man himself, to free him of the sorrows and pains, the frustrations and lusts by which he made himself and his fellows miserable.

These promises and hopes of the Renaissance, arising in the fourteenth century and achieving new forms and elaborations particularly in the seventeenth and eighteenth centuries, were sufficiently in accord with many actual achievements of history to defeat and overwhelm all the pessimistic scruples of the Reformation. The latter (partly indeed because they were too pessimistic and defeatist) maintained themselves only in the backwaters of modern civilization. All the basic beliefs of modern man about himself, his society, and his destiny were defined essentially by the Renaissance and by the various cultural movements that followed in its wake. Thinkers as diverse as Hegel and Marx participated in the general optimistic interpretation of human history. The latter did indeed believe that bourgeois society was moving toward catastrophe rather than triumph; but he was certain that an essentially perfect society would emerge from that catastrophe. Christianity itself, in its modern Protestant version, was strongly influenced by these optimistic interpretations of life and history. Some of the most stubborn and sentimental illusions about the possibilities of a simple and easy peace between the competing elements in human society have been fostered by modern churches. In America they contributed more possibly than any other influence to political and moral illusions, for they aggravated false estimates of man and history by compounding them with classical and pious conceptions.

The errors and illusions of our culture, which have made an estimate of the crisis of our civilization difficult if not impossible, are, almost without exception, various versions of a single error. They are all expressions of too great an optimism about the goodness of human nature; they all therefore underestimate the difficulties of relating life to life, will to will, interest to interest, in a harmonious social life. They regard the achievement of justice and social peace in human society as a comparatively easy task. It is, as a matter of fact, a very difficult task, which can be accomplished with tolerable success only if its difficulties are fully recognized.

Traditionalists are accustomed to criticize modern culture for the laxity of its moral standards. They think our primary sin is moral relativism and skepticism. Yet the moral relativism that denies the validity of all general norms of virtue and all universal standards of justice is really a subordinate note in modern culture. It has become dominant only in this latter day in Nazi philosophy and totalitarian politics. This philosophy proclaims unashamedly that there is no good but "my" good, and no standard of justice but the interest of "my" nation. This frank egoism, this cynical disregard of the interests of others, does indeed represent a final decay of moral standards. But it expresses itself as a revolt against our culture and civilization. It does not express the basic ideas of our culture.

Our culture in its dominant thought is neither skeptical nor cynical; neither relativist nor nihilistic. On the contrary, it has a touching confidence in the possibility of establishing "universal" standards of justice and general norms of value. It consistently underestimates the difficulties of achieving universal standards. It thinks that men can be beguiled from following their own interests and can be persuaded to espouse the general interest by some simple process of social reorganization or educational device.

Almost every version of modern culture has some futile and fatuous scheme for lifting men from selfish purposes as painlessly as possible. The simplest idea of all is that which underlies the laissez faire social philosophies of the eighteenth and nineteenth centuries. According to these philosophies all conflicting interests in human society, and all competing egoistic drives, would result in harmony rather than conflict if they were only left alone. If political society did not interfere with economic process, economic life would achieve a natural harmony. This idea, which obviates the necessity of either moral or political control upon selfish impulses, was a nice device for eating your cake and having it too. It justified unrestrained selfishness without justifying egoism morally; for it gave the assurance that "each man seeking his own would serve the commonweal." The only difficulty with the idea is that it is not true. The one element of truth in it is that there are indeed certain automatic harmonies in the economic process, and it is wise to maintain them. But on the whole, history, unlike nature, has no natural balances of power. Where power is disproportionate, power dominates weakness and injustice results. A technical civilization actually accentuates previous disproportions of power, so that the theory was less true for the growing technical society to which it was applied than for a more static agrarian society, to which it had not been applied.

The theory of the harmlessness of natural man, if only he is not controlled and regulated, is usually compounded with another theory, which is a little more profound. It is the theory that ignorant selfishness is dangerous to society, but that a wise and prudent selfishness knows how to relate the interests of the self to the interests of the whole; so that a wise egoist, while seeking his own pleasure, will finally serve "the greatest good of the greatest number." The confidence in the essential virtue of the intelligent man takes various forms. Sometimes intelligence supposedly restrains egoism in its narrow form and broadens it to include the interests of others. Sometimes it is assumed that the intelligence preserves a nice balance between egoistic and altruistic impulses. And sometimes reason throws the weight of its authority on the side of altruism as against egoism.

In the philosophy of Hegel, reason overcomes the narrow interests of the individual self by creating the state, as an expression of the broader interests of the collective self. Hegelian philosophy fails to consider, however, that human society is engulfed in conflict more frequently by competing collective wills than by conflicting individual wills and interests. The most tragic conflicts of history are between states, nations, classes, and races, and not between individuals.

The trust of the modern man in reason thus takes many forms. In all of them it assumes that reason is an organ of the universal and that in some way or other increasing reason will progressively remove conflict from human society and produce an ultimately perfect coincidence of interest with interest and a finally perfect conformity of will to will. Even Marxism, which is presumably a revolt against this trust in reason, is another version of the same faith. It assumes that nothing but the "class organization" of society tempts men to subordinate their reason to their passions and interests; and that the conflicts in human society will result in an ultimate catastrophe from which a new society will emerge in which there will be perfect harmony.

This trust in reason, as the organ of human virtue and as the guarantor of social peace and justice, underlies modern man's faith in history. For he conceives of history as a movement in which reason is progressively coming into control of all the vitalities, interests, and passions of life. If we are involved in conflict today we may therefore attribute it to the ignorance and the superstition of men; and look forward hopefully to the day when increasing education and advancing intelligence will have dispelled the bigotries of ignorant men and destroyed the parochialism of backward races and nations.

If the revolt against our civilization is to be understood profoundly and not merely attributed to the conspiracies of "bad" men, we must realize that totalitarian philosophy has in every case taken neglected portions of the total truth about man and history and fashioned them into perverse but potent instruments against a civilization that did not understand the nature and history of man. For the liberal faith in reason, Nazism substituted the romantic faith in vitality and force. For the simple faith that right creates its own might, it substituted the idea that might makes right. For the hope of liberal democracy that history was in the process of eliminating all partial, national, and racial loyalties and creating a universal community of mankind, it substituted a primitive loyalty to race and nation as the final end of life. In place of the sentimental idea that men could easily combine devotion to their own interests with loyalty to universal justice, it proclaimed the cynical idea that there is no justice but that which serves "my" or "our" purpose and interest.

It is wrong to worship force and to make power self-justifying. But such an error could not have arisen in a civilization that had not made the opposite mistake and assumed that men were in the process of becoming purely rational. It is perverse to make the interests of our nation the final end of life. But this error could not have achieved such monstrous proportions if our culture had not foolishly dreamed and hoped for the development of "universal" men, who were bereft of all loyalties to family, race, and nation. It is monstrous to glorify war as the final good. But that error could not have brought us so close to disaster if a comfortable civilization had not meanwhile regarded peace as a final good; and had not expected perfect peace to be an attainable goal of history. It is terrible to conduct the diplomacy and military strategy of nations upon the basis of "all or nothing" policies. But the fury expressed in such policies would have not come so close to success if it had not been met by the illusions of comfortable and fat nations in which the love of ease had been compounded with the caution of prudence, and the two together had resulted in an inability to act. If the lies embodied in the Nazi creed did not contain a modicum of truth and if that modicum of truth had not been directed against our weakness and our illusions, we would not have come so close to disaster.

We have defined the error that underlies all the optimistic illusions of our culture as a too-simple confidence in man, particularly in rational man, and as a too-simple hope in the progressive achievement of virtue in history, by reason of the progressive extension of intelligence. This confidence that human history ultimately answers all its unsolved problems and overcomes all its earlier insecurities, that history is itself a kind of process of redemption, has gained such a strong hold upon modern man because it is actually partly true and because all the tremendous advances of science, technology, and intelligence seemed to justify the belief. The Renaissance, which trusted in history, triumphed over the Reformation, which had serious questions about history, because we were actually making progress in so many directions that it seemed plausible to assume that all these advances could be summed up as moral progress. But this final conclusion represents a grievous error. There is always progress in history in the sense that it cumulates wisdom, perfects technics, increases the areas of human cooperation, and extends the human control over nature. But this cannot be regarded as moral progress. There are morally ambiguous elements in human history on every new level of achievement. We ought to have known that. A person progresses from childhood to maturity, but it is not easy to compare the virtue of maturity with the innocency of a child, because mature life achieves higher unities and is subject to greater complexities than child life. It is in fact irrelevant to measure mature virtue with childish innocency because they are incommensurate. So it is with the history of mankind.

The advancement of knowledge may mitigate social conflict, but intelligence may also be the servant of imperial ambition. The applied sciences and technics may multiply human power and increase comfort. But the Nazis may use the power for destructive ends; and the democratic world may be beguiled by the comforts of bourgeois society into a false security. Modern means of communication may increase the breadth and extent of human communities, but they also enlarge areas of human conflict. Reason may serve as an arbitrator between my interest and those of my fellowmen. In that case, reason is a servant of justice. But reason may, as Bergson observed, also break the communities of primitive life by giving the egoistic urge a new instrument.

Whether one analyzes the advances of history in terms of technics or of intelligence, it is quite apparent that history is not so simple as we have believed. The morally ambiguous note remains in it on every level. The securities of its maturity save us from the insecurities of childhood; but they do not save us from the new insecurities of maturity. The wisdom of maturity is a cure for the ignorance of childhood; but it is no cure for the ignorance of maturity. It is because we have trusted history too much that we understand neither life nor history. History cannot be the answer to our problems, for history is itself our problem. History is, in short, an inadequate god. We have failed to gauge every contemporary problem in its true depth because of this false faith in history. Previous civilizations only made the mistake of misjudging their own history and estimating their own security too highly. We went one step beyond them in pride and pretension. We thought no evil could befall us because we trusted not "Roman civilization" nor medieval culture, but history itself. Yet our error was greater than previous errors, precisely because we believed that history's development of all human potencies also guaranteed the elimination of all human insecurities. The very opposite is the truth. A highly dynamic technical society is more destructive in its decay than a simple agrarian society. The destruction dumped from the skies by modern airplanes is more awful than the lethal power of a bow and arrow.

And neither the further advance of science nor the mere return to religion will give us the perspective required. Neither return to a simpler piety nor advance from piety to a sophisticated scientific culture can solve our problem. Religious and scientific leaders may have been fighting each other, but they have shared the same common and erroneous faith. Neither were driven beyond the characteristic complacency of modern man in regard to history. The scientists may have regarded themselves as very sophisticated and thought of the religious people as very sentimental. But these superficial differences were insignificant. Scientists and pietists agreed in regarding human history as the answer to all human problems rather than as itself the great human problem.

If we seek for a cultural reconstruction in our day, we must look for something more fundamental than the mere extension of scientific knowledge, for science gives no answer to the ultimate problem of the meaning of life. Nor can we be satisfied with the conventional advice to return to religion. There must indeed be a return to religion in the sense that all final answers to ultimate problems are religious answers, whether clothed in the language and pretensions of science, philosophy, or religion. But a religious answer, per se, is no more adequate than a scientific answer. The Nazi answer to the problem of life is a religious answer; but Nazi religion is a primitive religion, which declares that the triumph of "my" nation fulfills the meaning of life and history. The Buddhist answer to the problem of life is a religious answer. But it declares that life is fulfilled by escape from history.

The primary significance of the Hebraic-Christian tradition, which underlies our Western culture, is that it regards historical existence as meaningful, but it sees no fulfillment of life's meaning in history, because it recognizes that history, on every level of achievement, contains ambiguities, problems, and insecurities that demand an answer. The answer to these problems given by the Christian faith is that history is borne by a divine reality that completes what remains incomplete in history and purges what is evil in history. This answer can be taken seriously only by those who recognize the seriousness of the problem to which it is an answer.

Our modern culture since the Renaissance has not taken the Christian faith seriously because it had a simpler answer to the problems of life. It agreed with Christianity in regarding human history as meaningful, but it assigned a simple meaning to history. The Reformation was meanwhile overwhelmed because it was too pessimistic about the possibilities of history.

An adequate faith for our day must again combine these broken fragments of the Christian tradition. Any culture or any religion that is deficient in the "tragic sense of life" is certainly inadequate to give us light and guidance in a day in which the very securities of a technical society have been transmuted into evil. We need a faith that throws light upon the importance of every historical task and responsibility. But it must on the other hand reveal the limits of all historical striving. Without such a faith, the modern man remains an inveterate utopian, disavowing all religious ultimates in one breath and in the next breath affirming his faith in some incredible utopia, some impossible heaven on earth.

An adequate religious culture must transcend the stabilities, securities, achievements of any given civilization. If faith is bound up with these too completely, life becomes meaningless when they break down. It must give people the resource to rebuild a civilization without illusions and yet without despair. We must, for instance, achieve a higher level of international organization after the war or our civilization will sink even lower. If we engage in the task of world reconstruction without a disavowal of the utopian illusion, which has informed our culture particularly since the eighteenth century, we shall ask for the impossible by way of world federation or some world superstate; we shall not get it, and then we shall be tempted again to despair and disillusionment. Furthermore, the utopians will always tempt the realists among us to become cynical in their reaction to utopianism. These cynics will be inclined to assert that history contains no new possibilities for good. They will seek to reconstruct the world on the basis of the old precarious balance of power, and they will not find a new level of international community compatible with our new economic interdependence.

All political and economic achievements must be informed by a religion and a culture, which know that history is a realm of infinite possibilities, and that each new level of maturity places new responsibilities upon us. But it must also be understood that all historic achievements are limited and precarious; that human egoism, individual and collective, can be transmuted and sublimated on many new levels, but that it cannot be eliminated from history. The faith that man as a particular force in history, contending against other particular forces, is in the process of becoming a universal force, has no historical evidence to justify it. The modern man regards himself as so sophisticated and is nevertheless incredibly credulous. Human existence is precarious and will remain so to the end of history. Human achievement contains a tragic element of frustration and corruption and will contain it to the end of history. There is an ultimate answer to these tragic aspects of human existence, but that answer can be known only to those who have stopped looking for some easy escape from tragedy.

The Christian religion regards history as meaningful but as having no fulfillment of its meaning within itself. In that sense Christianity is "otherworldly." For this reason all modern substitutes for the Christian faith, in which history is fulfilled in some kind of utopia, naturally find the Christian faith incredible because they have a simpler answer to the problems of life. The Christian faith becomes credible only when those simpler answers are refuted by history, as indeed they are bound to be.

According to the Christian faith all finite and historical existence points to a ground and an end beyond itself. This divine end and ground is paradoxically defined as having a double relation to history. God judges the world because there are violations of the law of life on every level of human achievement. God "saves" the world because he has resources of mercy beyond his judgment. But mercy cannot express itself without taking justice seriously. Thus God is pictured as being able to be merciful only by taking the consequences of his judgment upon and into himself. These paradoxes of the Christian faith have sometimes been stated in terms of a wooden literalism that has made them offensive to human intelligence. But it is well to remember that they are a "stumbling block" and "foolishness" even when stated profoundly. The reason for this is that all men would like to believe that they have the power within themselves to complete their lives and their history. But this is exactly what all men lack.

A faith that is able to transcend the catastrophes of history must therefore be able to define both the possibilities of human creativity in history and the limits of human possibilities. It must also be able to clarify the fact that the evils of fanaticism, conflict, imperialism, and tyranny have their source in man's ambition to overleap his limitations and to seek unconditioned power, virtue, and security for his existence.

For this reason historical catastrophe seems to be nothing but chaos, which drives men to despair without the profundities of the Christian faith. And Christian faith becomes vapid and sentimental in periods of stability and peace. It recovers its own profoundest insights precisely in those periods of social chaos when all simpler interpretations of life break down and force men to seek for a profounder interpretation of existence.

The God of History

[*The Messenger,* Vol. 18 (February 10, 1953), pp. 6–7.] From 1946 to 1957 Niebuhr wrote a column carried by three denominational magazines, *Episcopal Churchnews, The Lutheran,* and *The Messenger*—the latter a publication of the Evangelical and Reformed Church, now part of the United Church of Christ, to which he belonged. This piece, and five others reprinted in this anthology, appeared in that column.

A PRINCETON professor, who recently shocked the religious world by an essay in which he sought to prove that science invalidated religion, has now written a book in which he affirms that, while science may analyze the natural order, the mystic experience penetrates to the eternal, rather than the temporal, dimension of existence; that science and religion are therefore not incompatible. The book will be received with appreciation by many, but it indicates an interesting trend among intellectuals which will seem significant from the standpoint of the Christian faith, whether it is Aldous Huxley or Professor Stace.

When intellectuals become religious they are more likely to embrace mysticism than Christianity. The former affirms the reality of the eternal world, but it insists that nothing specific can be affirmed about it, as the definitions are all negative. They say what God is not. "To name God is to blaspheme him," declared a renowned mystic. The Christian faith on the other hand "names" God and declares that the mystery of the divine, while inscrutable to human intelligence, is disclosed by a series of historical events in which God reveals his character, will, and purpose.

Christianity, in short, is a historical-dramatic religion in which the ultimate truth is revealed in a drama in the course of history. It is to be distinguished from those religions and philosophies which discern the ultimate truth in some structure of nature or reason, or in some unfathomable mystery. It is naturally not so "rational" as these other faiths, but that is not to say that it is irrational.

The ultimate verification of the truth of the Christian faith depends upon the ability of our faith to illumine everything which pertains to the realm of personality, whether human or divine. In the realm of persons, verification is different than in the realm of things. Persons relate themselves to each other by faith and love and not by being fitted into some scheme or system. In the realm of persons, unique events and attitudes are dramatically correlated.

In the realm of things, there is no room for unique events but only for events which follow inevitably and necessarily from the essential nature of those things. Thus in a scientific age the Christian faith is embarrassed because it is rooted in a unique historical event, the coming of Christ; and it affirms God's freedom as a Person, while scientific and philosophical speculation never reaches the point of affirming the selfhood of God. We have, in fact, the ironic circumstance that the God we know purely by our reason is something less than God because he is an impersonal divinity. "If thou canst comprehend Him," declares St. Augustine, "He is not God."

The Two Sources of Western Culture

[*The Christian Idea of Education,* edited by Edmund Fuller (New Haven: Yale University Press, 1957), pp. 237–54.] At a seminar at the Kent School in Connecticut in 1955, Niebuhr delivered this paper on the Hellenic and Hebraic roots of Western culture.

I

IT may well be that the dynamic superiority of Western culture, with its sense of the importance of history and with its conquest of natural forces, has its origin and source in the double root of our culture, the Hellenic and the Hebraic. Each supplied a necessary tool for the definition of the meaning of human existence which every culture seeks to supply. Thus the two facets of meaning were more adequately supplied than in other cultures, which were either too rational or too mystical to define the meaning of existence in terms which would do justice to the unity and the richness and variety of life.

The meaning of existence is established on the one hand by the order and coherence of our world. We establish meaning by any theoretic and practical pursuits which display the coherence, the causal sequences, and the dependabilities of our existence and our world. But pure order would destroy the meaning of human existence insofar as our existence displays the freedom of the person, his responsibility, his capacity to transcend the sequences and necessities of nature, to elaborate a realm of history which is not simply rational because it is not governed by either metaphysical or natural necessity but contains configurations in which freedom and necessity are variously compounded.

Furthermore, human life contains various corruptions of man's freedom, man's sins in short, for which either there is no answer or the answer must be the divine grace of which the Bible speaks. The grace of God as a final answer to the human problem points to God's freedom, which can be comprehended as little in a rational system as the freedom, the responsibility, and the sin of man.

In short, the realm of meaning has dimensions of both order and freedom, and every culture seeks to do justice to these two dimensions. The religious element in a culture is the capstone of the realm of meaning. It furnishes the framework for the structure of meaning and states the ultimate principle and power which is presupposed in that structure.

Western culture is unique in human history in that it draws upon two different sources for its conceptions of meaning, the Hebraic and the Hellenic. Each of these sources has the capacity to do justice to one of the dimensions of meaning and is defective in comprehending the other, but the two together comprehend both natural and historical reality more adequately than any other culture. The Greeks were gifted philosophers, metaphysicians, and mathematicians who were consistently seeking for the rational coherence of things. Their metaphysical speculations laid the foundation not only for modern philosophy but for modern science insofar as science is derived from the rational analysis of causes, particularly of efficient cause. The Greeks were not predominantly naturalistic. The atomists and Epicureans were vanquished by Platonists, Aristotelians, and Stoics; and this triumph proves that they were more interested in the ultimate issues of meaning than in the analysis of efficient cause. Since then the Hellenic component of our culture has tended more and more to naturalistic metaphysics as the project of understanding nature and harnessing her resources became the preoccupation of our culture and its success in doing so gave the determinisms, which were the by-product of the understanding of nature, unusual prestige.

It would be untrue and unfair to say that we derived our science from the Greeks and our religion from the Hebrews. The Greeks combined a strong religious impulse with their metaphysical impulse. Aristotle's God was the rational structure of all existing reality.

Nor were the Greeks uninterested in the ethical problem, so that it would not be right to suggest that we have our moral heritage from the Hebrews rather than the Greeks. Our moral heritage combines Greek and Hebraic elements. Morality meant for the Greeks conformity to the pattern of existence. The political constitution of the *polis* sought to imitate the basic order of the universe. Hence Aristotle emphasized the importance of the constitution of the polis as a source of civic virtue. All natural law concepts in Western history are certainly drawn from the Greek idea of a basic structure or form of life to which human actions must conform. These structures were elaborated primarily in Aristotelian and Stoic thought. The common law tradition of England, in particular, with its sense of an historic accommodation of the vitalities and interests of a community, on the other hand, is certainly more Hebraic than Hellenic, though the Greeks had an interest in historically established norms.

It is not true therefore that we drew our religion and ethics from the Hebrews and our philosophy and science from the Greeks. It is true that every conception of meaning which depends upon structure, plan, or scheme is Greek in origin. But all dimensions of meaning which seek to incorporate the freedom of God and man, the uniqueness and wholeness of the person in body and soul, the responsibility which is derived from human freedom, the sin which is a corruption of that freedom, the historical configurations which men elaborate above the level of natural necessity, and the assurance of divine grace to the repentant sinner are derived from Hebrew sources.

Hebraic religion avails itself of poetic and historical symbols for the suggestions and revelations of ultimate meaning. These symbols suggest both mystery and specific meaning rather than the Greek identification of meaning with rational intelligibility. God, the God of the Bible, is the mysterious Creator of the world. He is mysterious because creation transcends all concepts of efficient or formal cause. Creation is beyond comprehension, a fact which Christian theology finally spells out in its concept of "*Creatio ex nihilo.*" But the God of the Bible is the Creator of the world, only, as it were, as an afterthought in the theory of the prophets. The creation of the world is ascribed to Him to affirm that this God with whom Israel has to do is the God above all gods, the supreme God, and not an idol of a nation. God is comprehended in the first instance as the sovereign of history, who reigns over the destiny of all peoples but who has called Israel to a special mission among the people. The fact that He has done this is, according to Deuteronomy, inexplicable. God's covenant grace is in fact as inscrutable as creation. No reason can be given for His acts. These acts are the basis upon which we build all our structures of meaning. The God of the Bible is revealed not so much in the permanent structures of life through which history flows as in the "mighty acts," the particular events of history which point beyond themselves to the ultimate ground and the mystery and meaning which give significance to our existence.

Insofar as the Christian faith is grounded in the Bible it is Hebraic rather than Hellenic. It is a faith in which revelation appears in history and in which the revelation imparts specific meaning to the mystery of the divine without annulling the mystery. His thoughts are not our thoughts and His ways not our ways, yet He is not complete mystery. We know of His mercy and of His righteousness and of the paradoxical relation between His righteousness and mercy. The Pope is right that "spiritually we are all Semites," even though the Christian community is founded upon a revelation that the Jews rejected and that to the Christian represents the supreme and final revelation in which the obscurities of all prophetic intimations of the divine are clarified. A man appears in history who is at the same time the second Adam and the revelation of a divine mercy. The Agape incarnate in his life is the norm of human existence which is approximated but not fully realized in all human history. When it is realized in history it ends upon the Cross, a symbol of the fact that the norms of human history transcend the actual course of history. But the Christian community discerns by a miracle of grace that this death upon the Cross is not pure tragedy. It is also a revelation of the love of a suffering God Who takes the frustrations and contradictions and sins of man in history upon and unto Himself. That is the only possibility of finally overcoming the corruptions of human freedom which will express themselves in history until the end, and more particularly at the end (the anti-Christ), for human freedom over nature constantly develops and with it the possibilities of both good and evil. The Christian faith is not the guarantee that good will triumph over evil in history. It is a summons to responsible action in history based upon the assurance that evil will not finally triumph over God's designs. According to St. Paul, those who have not this key to the mystery of life and of God are tempted either to sleep or be drunken, to be either complacent or hysterical when confronted with the evils of history. But those who have the key are enabled to watch and be sober.

II

If we analyze the task of transmitting this faith, grounded in this revelation, as a source of grace amidst the confusions in our own day, we must be clear about the hazards which accompany the task both perennially and specifically in our day.

We must begin with the perennial embarrassments of this faith which Paul acknowledges so boldly. It is to the Jews a stumbling block and to the Greeks foolishness. It embodies the scandal of particularity, of "*Einmaligkeit.*" It asserts that the ultimate mystery and meaning have been finally and definitively revealed in one person and in one drama of history. That is foolishness to the Greeks who are trying to discern a key to the meaning of life by penetrating through the flow of events in history to the structures which bear it. This faith, in contrast, asserts and affirms that the key is in a mysterious divine power in which creative and redemptive power are paradoxically united, and in which there is freedom to come to terms with all the exigencies of history, embodying the freedom of a curious creature who is called to be a creator even though he is a creature, and who invariably uses his freedom not only to create but to destroy. The affirmation upon which the Christian Church is founded is also "a stumbling block to the Jews" because it does not simply assert the triumph of the divine power over all evil in history. It affirms that the divine power cannot triumph without becoming involved in the evil and suffering of history. It asserts the absurdity of a "suffering

God" rather than a triumphant God, of a God revealed in a man who uttered a cry of despair before his ultimate triumph, and thus gave an indication of how close meaninglessness and chaos are to the triumph of faith.

The essential message of the Bible, particularly in this final climax of revelation, triumphed over the Greek culture and embodied some of the wisdom of the Greeks in its system. It triumphed over the wisdom of the Greeks because, as St. Paul affirmed, it embodied the "foolishness of God which is wiser than men," because it gave a more ultimate and satisfying, above all a more redemptive, answer to the enigma of human existence than the wisdom of the Greeks. It did this because the wisdom of the Greeks had no place for the mystery of divine and human freedom, including the mystery of sin in human freedom and the mystery of divine grace in divine freedom.

But the triumph of Christianity over Greek culture did not obviate the necessity of coming to terms with the wisdom incorporated in that culture, beginning with the Johannine literature of the Bible and continuing through the efforts at synthesis from Augustine to Thomas Aquinas. The reason for this inevitable synthesis is simple. The world of both nature and history embodies structures, continuities, plans and forms, essences and entelechies which must be analyzed scientifically and metaphysically. The metaphysical analyses search for the rational structure of things above the level of efficient cause. Therefore a culture which emphasizes only freedom, contingency, and uniqueness as the Hebraic does cannot come to terms with the whole dimension of existence. The Christian faith is primarily Hebraic and does not simply compound Hebraic and Hellenic viewpoints. But it does embody Hellenic viewpoints beginning with the Johannine conception of Christ as the Logos Who is the pattern of creation and of love as an old law and a new law. It is an old law in the sense that it is the only possible law for man who is free to surpass himself but must find himself in going out from himself to the neighbor and to God. It is a new law, revealed by Christ in the sense that this law is historically illumined and clarified and its full import cannot be revealed in any structure of creation. For man has the freedom to surpass his created structure, being both creature and creator.

In dealing with the Christian content of our Western culture and the possibility of transmitting it in education, we must analyze why this subordinate Hellenic element achieved such undue emphasis in our own latter day, why it became rather un-Greek in its tendency toward a naturalistic metaphysic, and why just when these tendencies had reached their climax the historic situation required the full force of the wisdom and grace of the Christian Gospel and particularly that part of it which transcended the wisdom of the Greeks.

There are many reasons which we must enumerate for the triumph of the Greek element in our culture over the Hebraic-Christian one.

Undoubtedly the most important cause of the gradual triumph of the Greek component in our culture over the Hebraic-Christian one must be sought in the interest of modern man, particularly since the seventeenth century, in the laws and causalities of nature and in the prestige of modern science's "conquest of nature." Nature is a realm of necessity, and its meanings can therefore be equated with rational intelligibility, particularly with rational, analyzable, efficient, and natural causes rather than the realm of history in which freedom and necessity are so curiously compounded. The very triumphs of modern science not only accentuated the Greek interest in structures but guided modern culture to deterministic and naturalistic versions of these structures, which are not characteristically Greek but are the natural by-product of preoccupations with efficient cause in which the irrationality of the givenness of things, the mystery of freedom and creation, is naturally obscured by the principle of science "Ex nihilo nihil sit." There are, of course, many sequences and causal coherences in human history and therefore scientific elements in historiography. But it is significant that the meaning of historical events has frequently been obscured not by the real historian but by social scientists who sought abortively to bring history into the realm of nature and thus deny the characteristically historical aspects of the human scene. In short, our culture has been intent upon equating history with nature at the precise moment when history revealed the dangerous possibilities of human freedom which were not at all like nature.

Secondly, the triumph of the Hellenic component over the Hebraic must be attributed to the inexactness of the pictorial and historical symbols of meaning in comparison with the scientific and metaphysical ones. This inexactness contains temptations toward arbitrariness and to obscurantism in culture.

The obscurantist corruptions of religion became particularly apparent in the nineteenth century when the Biblical idea of creation was used to challenge the scientific scrutiny into the chronology of the causal sequences in the time process and to set faith against the undoubted fact of natural evolution. But there were many less vivid but not less influential contests between obscurantist versions of the Christian faith and the scientific world view. The general effect of these contests was to persuade the modern generation that it was inevitable that religious people should have confused the permanent and necessary myths and symbols of religion, which indicate some transtemporal meaning or reality in the terms of the temporal, with prescientific myth which was a collection of symbols elaborated by the human imagination before modern science elaborated the picture of the world as governed by laws, sequences, and coherences.

We cannot fruitfully reverse the process of the past centuries and give a new dignity to the Hebraic-Christian component of our culture without working out to the last conclusion every problem which has been projected by the difference between religious and scientific symbols; and without admitting the obscurantist dangers in the use of the religious symbols.

Those of us engaged in education need only think of the heritage of suspicion which the age of warfare between science and religion has left as a deposit in the minds of the younger generation to be reminded that there can be no simple return to religion even in a catastrophic age without solving the problem of doing justice to the divine freedom, and without annulling the well-established fact that the universe is law-abiding and that we may even speak of "laws" in the realm of human history where freedom and necessity are so variously compounded.

The third reason for the decay of the Hebraic-Christian component in our culture is one which must be humbly acknowledged by the religiously inclined because it has to do with the religious value of ostensible irreligion. Our age is an irreligious one in the sense that preponderant opinion in our culture rejects the idea of a divine mystery and sovereignty within and beyond the observable phenomena of the world. It regards the world as self-explanatory and life as self-fulfilling. It may have various versions of its rejection of the God of the Bible, either naturalistic or idealistic. The God of the Bible is suspect not only because He is a suffering God (which was an offense to ancient Greeks) but because He is declared to be a person. (That is an offense to the modern Greeks.) The symbol of personality, however subject to distortion, is the only adequate description of the combination of freedom and structure in the divine life. This is an added case of permanent myth being involved in the prescientific myths of the divine, of the childish myths which picture God as an old man with a beard. The fact is that religion points to the ultimate ground of our existence and to the ultimate purpose of all our striving. It is therefore dangerous because every historic form of faith, including those in which idolatry has been overcome in principle, is bound to dignify some partial human value or end or center of meaning with the ultimate ground. There are, in short, idolatrous elements in all historic expressions of faith which make it impossible to identify belief in God with all virtue and agnosticism with vice. We must guard against all pretentious affirmations which equate piety with virtue if we would participate in the revival of religious faith. In the words of the great French Catholic theologian Delacroix, "There are wrong and right ways of believing in God," and much of modern atheism was in its inception a protest against corrupt forms of piety. The atheism of both the bourgeois and the Marxist movements was partly rooted in materialistic misconceptions and partly in an ethical impulse, the impulse to challenge the religious support of historic forms of injustice, the defense of particular human interest in the name of God.

We are all familiar with the intimate relation between medieval forms of the

Christian faith and the feudal structure of society which was partly responsible (though only partly) for the atheism of the French Enlightenment and for the conviction of Diderot that injustice would be abolished if only "priests and their hypocritical tools" could be banished. We know of the moral scruples which prompted the atheism of the Russian nihilists, precursors of modern Communists, and know of the intimate relation between Protestant forms of piety and bourgeois forms of culture, and of the effort to support the interest of the latter by the prestige of the former.

Atheism in its more pristine forms usually contained an effort to guard disinterest against religiously sanctified interests. This did not, of course, prevent interests from availing themselves of scientific prestige for the guarding of their cherished values or prevent the worst form of theocracy from arising on the soil of atheistic Communism. The human heart, particularly the heart dominated by self-love, is full of guile; and it is able to use every instrument of religion and irreligion to sanctify its interests. The instruments most serviceable to it are those which have a contemporary prestige of disinterestedness.

The complexities of these involvements of the search for the ultimate with immediate interests must be understood if we would not fall into some naïve hope that the revival of the Christian faith will purge the world of evil.

We are living in a secularized Christian culture, and there are those who believe that all current evils are derived from secularism. They point to Communism as the final fruit of secularism, which is about as logical as to regard clerical absolutism as the logical and only fruit of Christianity. The fact is that secularism, as the natural consequence of a disavowal of the holy and an indifference toward ultimate issues and ends of life, creates its own problems, including preoccupation with the immediate ends of life or the covert glorification of some immediate end as the ultimate end of human existence. We may regard the current preoccupation in America with technics and with the resultant productivity and wealth as an example of the first weakness. Communism, with it religious fanaticism without benefit of clergy, is an example of the second. The emergence of Communism in a secular age does prove that an explicit disavowal of the holy is no proof against the emergence of false sanctities in history.

But these weaknesses of secular cultures must not obscure the fact that explicitly religious cultures are subject to the errors of profanity or the corruption of the holy. It is interesting that "secular" and "profane" originally had almost identical connotations. Yet the different connotations which have developed in our language about these two words are instructive. The fact that there can be both corruption of the holy and indifference toward it must prevent both religious and nonreligious thinkers from drawing too simple conclusions about the virtues and vices of either religion or irreligion.

III

But despite the corruption within the religious cultures of the past, including our own, we are undoubtedly confronting the disintegration of the confident secularism of our era and a return to various forms of historic Christian and Jewish faith. The reasons for this return are many and various. The most obvious reason is the shock of the appearance of a secularized form of fanaticism and cruelty in the Communist movement. But there are more basic reasons for the disintegration of secularism. They are connected with the refutation by current history of the most cherished beliefs of a culture which ostensibly lived without beliefs, at least without beliefs having to do with the meaning of our existence. But modern culture proved that such a religious vacuum was bound to be filled. It was filled by various credos. But these different forms of secularized religion, which gave ultimate answers to the problem of human existence under the guise of giving immediate answers to immediate problems, can be reduced finally to two beliefs: to the idea of progress, which was the effective religion of the bourgeois world, and to the Marxist creed, which was the creed of the class of industrial workers. Their experience did not allow them to indulge in the simple optimism of the middle class world. An immediately pessimistic and ultimately optimistic interpretation of history, which predicted social catastrophe, and salvation emerging out of the social catastrophe, seemed more plausible to the workers or to the intellectuals, who regarded themselves as the surrogates for the workers. History has refuted both religions. That is, in a nutshell, the cause of the spiritual crisis of our age.

The idea of progress arose in the Renaissance and reached its climax in the nineteenth and early twentieth centuries. It was fed by many streams of thought, but two elaborations of the Hellenic component in our culture contributed particularly to the idea, which was after all quite un-Hellenic in its contrast to the Greek conception of a cyclical history. The one was confidence in human reason as the source of virtue, which was changed under modern impacts into confidence in man's increasing rationality or rational competence. In this sense the idea of progress resulted from the merger of the modern optimism with the Greek confidence in reason or in the identification of man's reason with his highest self.

The other root of the idea of progress was the modern conquest of nature based upon the Hellenic idea of an inherent rationality of nature, which made it subject to rational inquiry according to its rational coherences, and upon the Biblical idea of the incomprehensible givenness of things in creation, without which modern empiricism, inductive rather than deductive analysis could not have arisen. We are all familiar with the story of modern science's "conquest" of nature which has so altered the whole human situation that it seemed for a time as if it had altered it even more radically than it had and as if it had made man the master not only of nature but of his own destiny. The vision of human reason's elimination of ancient stupidities and superstitions and the hope of the conquest of nature to the point where human weakness would be completely overcome, these two hopes lie at the foundation of the modern idea of progress which became the effective religion of modern man, imparting meaning to this existence and promising him redemption from every evil.

The idea of progress has been refuted by the tragic events of current history. We have global wars instead of the parliament of mankind and the federation of the world. Cruel tyrannies have emerged in an era in which democracy and liberty were expected to be triumphant. And the world's enmities became the more tragic since science had given the weapons of warfare a new destructiveness through the discoveries of nuclear physics. History refuted the hopes of the past centuries because they were founded upon two erroneous beliefs. The one was that reason could be the master of interest and passion and therefore the instrument of increasingly universal interests. This was an error since reason is always intimately related to the self and is more easily the servant than the master of the self.

The other error was derived from the first. It was the mistaken belief that every triumph over nature and every consequent enhancement of human freedom would redound to the benefit of man. The error lay in regarding man's freedom over nature as unambiguously good. Yet all human freedom contains the possibilities of both creativity and destructiveness. Human history is therefore bound to develop in both dimensions to its end. Our generation has had tragic and vivid displays of this truth in the good and evil, in the increasing community, and in the increasingly lethal warfare in our experience. Thus contemporary history has refuted the too simple interpretations which have been given to both life and history by modern secularized religions. It is rather ironic that the Marxist alternative to the liberal idea of progress was closer to the Biblical apocalyptic views than were the progressive notions. It had a conception of judgment and redemption which embodied some of the paradoxes of Biblical faith. But it was even more grievously mistaken in its utopian visions than the liberal alternative, for it generated hell on earth through its dreams of heaven on earth.

It is the refutation of the "wisdom of the world" in contemporary experience and the proof that these simple explanations of the meaning of our existence are really "foolishness" which give the Christian faith new relevance in our day. The foolishness of redemption through the suffering God, the absurdity of the affirmation that we must die to self if we would truly live, the scandal of the claim that the mystery of the divine has been revealed in an historical drama and that this drama gives us the key to the ultimate mysteries, all these claims were so easily dismissed by previous generations and yet seem so much more plausible to this generation.

IV

Before engaging in the task of examining the relevance of the Christian faith in a day which has witnessed the refutation of alternative wisdoms, it will be necessary to clarify one point of apparent obscurity. It would seem as if we had identified what is known as modern secularism with the Greek component of our culture, and the religious impulse toward ultimate ends and answers to the riddle of existence with the Hebraic component. Put thus baldly, the correlation would be erroneous. Hellenism was certainly not defective in its sense of the ultimate, at least not in the thought of Plato, Aristotle, and the Stoics. Furthermore the two dominant tendencies in the credo of modern secularism, namely a naturalistic metaphysics and a progressive interpretation of the drama of history, were both in conflict with classical Hellenism. A naturalistic ontology was vanquished in the classical culture, and the idea of progress was a secularized version of the Biblical idea of a dynamic history rather than a fruit of Greek philosophy of history which was consistently cyclical in its interpretation.

Yet there is some justice in this correlation between secularism and the Greek component if it is recognized that both credos of modern culture grew up on the ground of a thoroughly Greek understanding of the rationality of the world, and both sought to reduce the meaning of life to the dimension of rational intelligibility, banishing mystery from the realm of meaning. Nature is reduced to intelligibility by explaining its events in terms merely of natural or efficient cause. And history is made simply intelligible if it is regarded as a projection of nature and if its events are seen as determined by some rational principle of movement toward a goal. In either case the mystery of freedom, particularly the freedom of man in history, is obscured. If this freedom is granted, the realm of history is immediately filled with realities which are not easily correlated in a rational scheme. Among these are particularly the incomprehensible individual and the seemingly capricious historical configuration in which human freedom and natural necessity are variously compounded.

The modern man is as defective as the classical Greek in both his comprehension of the mysteries of selfhood and the mysteries and meanings of the endless and baffling configurations of the dramas of human history. These meanings can be apprehended only by taking the responsible freedom of man seriously, even though that freedom is always partially conditioned and obscured by the various determinisms of nature and of history in which man as a creature is involved. The freedom of man also introduces another factor into the realm of meaning which cannot be easily digested in a rational system, namely his sin and guilt. There is no balm for this sin in any purely rational system but only in the assurance that there is an ultimate divine freedom of grace rising above the intelligible structures of the cosmos. Furthermore, the freedom of man—his capacity to rise above the temporal flux in which he is so obviously involved—faces him with the problem of his death and the possibility of any abidingness of his own life in the flux of time and decay. The various configurations of the historical drama can be rationally correlated on various levels, and we can speak of the rise and decline of this or that civilization of a bourgeois culture and a feudal structure.

If we look at the total human drama, we can find no conclusion within it but only the perplexing development of both good and evil possibilities. History most surely points beyond itself for the completion of its meanings and these completions can only be apprehended by faith rather than by reason. This is why the Biblical-Hebraic faith must remain the bearer of the religious content of our culture. The faith of the Bible seeks to penetrate the mysteries and meanings of life above and beyond the rational intelligibilities. It is not for this reason "otherworldly." Rather it has a firm grasp upon the meanings of life in history and does not reduce them to meaninglessness by seeking to comprehend them too simply into some realm of rationality. "Deeper than life the plan of life doth lie."

A too simple insistence on rational intelligibility on the other hand is always in danger of reducing life to a dimension in which the very realities which give life meaning, freedom and responsibility, self-transcendence and the love of the neighbor, the grace which empowers the self to love and overcomes its sin, all these realities or dimensions of reality are denied.

But we cannot conclude a consideration of the revival of the Christian faith without considering the task which our generation, like all Christian generations, must confront anew. That is the task of relating freedom to the structures and essences of life and of correlating faith to reason. Without this task religious faith degenerates into obscurantism, and the Christian faith remains separated from modern culture and is available only to those who are too ignorant to know of the problem of the relation of God's and man's freedom to the various structures and cohesions and coherences of the cosmos. This is a formidable task in the pursuit of which we must undoubtedly avail ourselves of the help of modern process philosophies in place of the synthesis between the Christian faith and Aristotelian philosophy which was effected in the Middle Ages.

The task can be accomplished only if Christians have on the one hand a sure grasp of the wisdom of God which is contained in the foolishness of the Gospel, and on the other a humble recognition of the validity of the wisdoms of the world on their own level—namely, when they are charting and analyzing any coherence or structure of nature or of history in which rational analysis is a guide to the truth about life.

Fragments

ON FAITH AND PRESENT TASKS

We have lived so long in a culture which drew the meaning of our moral responsibilities from the hope of their actual fulfillment in history, that Christians, as well as non-Christians, are poorly prepared for the insecurities of our present existence. "Be not anxious for tomorrow," declared Jesus, "for tomorrow will be anxious for the things of itself; sufficient unto the day are the evils thereof." This warning suggests that our tasks and responsibilities have an intrinsic and absolute validity in God's sight in the present moment without too much regard for their historic fulfillment and justification.

"The Nonchalance of Faith," *Christianity and Society*, Vol. 11 (Winter 1945), p. 9.

ON THE PROVIDENCE OF GOD

The Biblical faith in the providence of God must again triumph over man's sense of omnipotence before we can act with a proper sense of proportion. Either there is no pattern of history at all (in which case a cosmic caprice will finally destroy every sense of the meaning of life); or there is a pattern but it is beyond our comprehension and under a Sovereignty which we can only dimly discern.

"Providence and Human Decisions," *Christianity and Crisis*, Vol. 8 (January 24, 1949), p. 185.

ON SOCIAL JUSTICE IN BIBLICAL FAITH

It is fortunate that the Old Testament expresses the religious concern for social justice. It has been a great resource in preventing a purely individual interpretation of the Christian faith.

"The Moral and Political Judgments of Christians," *Christianity and Crisis*, Vol. 19 (July 6, 1959), p. 100.

PART II
SOCIAL PHILOSOPHY

Will Civilization Survive Technics?

[*Commentary*, Vol. 1 (December 1945), pp. 1–8.]

THE diagnosticians of a historical crisis usually see one or the other dimension of the crisis. They see either the political-social maladjustments in the body of civilization, or the philosophical-religious weaknesses in the spirit of a culture; and attribute our difficulties solely to the one or to the other. This is analogous to a neurologist and a psychiatrist cooperating in the diagnosis of a patient and creating confusion because the one attributes his illness to purely physical, and the other to purely psychic causes.

There have, for instance, been many diagnoses of the collapse of France in which the defeat of France has been attributed to a variety of causes, spiritual and physical, running all the way from the effect of eighteenth-century philosophy upon French morale, through the disintegration of the French family, and ending with technical aspects of French military inadequacy. All of these diagnoses may have been true on their own level. But no one has sought to present a theory of breakdown which would bring all the diagnoses into a consistent whole.

The present crisis in our culture and our civilization is certainly wide and deep enough to involve, and probably to have been caused by maladjustments on all levels of our existence.

On the political and economic level the situation is fairly clear. Our crisis is due to the fact that we have not been able to develop political and social instruments which are adequate for the kind of a society which a technical civilization makes possible and necessary. The atomic bomb is in a sense only the most recent and the most dramatic symbol of this deep inner contradiction which cleaves our whole society. The ever increasing introduction of technics into the fields of production and communications constantly enlarges the intensity and extent of social cohesion in modern man's common life; and also tends constantly to centralize effective economic power. The effect of technics upon communications is to create a potential world community, which we have not been able to actualize morally and politically. The effect of technics upon production is to create greater and greater disproportions of economic power and thus to make the achievement of justice difficult. The one represents the international aspect of our crisis and the other the domestic aspect. We might well consider each in turn.

On the level of international life Nazism was a form of tyranny which grew in the soil of international anarchy and sought to overcome that anarchy by the coerced unification of the world. Had not the several nations felt themselves irresponsible toward the duty of maintaining the liberties of each against the threat of aggression, Nazism could not have come within an ace of achieving success. Nations have not, of course, ever accepted a very high degree of responsibility for each other's welfare. But modern technics had created a world-community in embryo. It was by the use of modern technics that one nation could gain the military power to make world-domination a plausible military goal. It therefore became necessary to develop political instruments through which the nations of the world would express and implement a worldwide sense of common responsibility. Since it was not possible to take such a step quickly the tyrannical threat almost succeeded.

Indeed it is still far from certain even now that we will have adequate instruments, or a sufficiently universal moral sense, to solve the problems of community on a worldwide scale. The political instruments that have been constructed at the San Francisco Conference are obviously of only minimal efficacy for the purposes for which they are intended. They could not be made much better because of a lack in the moral imagination of the nations. Each of the great powers is still more interested in strategic security for the event of another conflict than it is in security against conflict.

The systems of unilateral security which have been more or less artfully combined with a general system of mutual security may very easily vitiate the power of the mutual system. We have, for this reason, no right to hope that we are at the end of the crisis of our age on the level of the international problem.

It is possible indeed that we may live in this crisis for centuries. The task of building a genuine world-community is greater than any generation can solve; and it may be too great for the resources of a century. The enormity of the task is usually underestimated. Our cultural presuppositions are such that we have not understood the tragic character of history or the difficulty of historic achievements.

The present-day world community is held together by economic interdependence created by modern technics; and is threatened by the technical elaboration of instruments of warfare. The forces which make for political and moral cohesion are minimal. They consist of a general though rather vague sense of universal moral obligation; and of the fear of the consequences of overt world-anarchy.

This fear of war is however not as potent a cement of cohesion as the fear of a concrete foe, which has frequently welded smaller communities together. Furthermore the international community lacks all the intermediate forms of cohesion that hold national and imperial communities together. It lacks a single center of power and authority, a common language or a common cultural, moral, or religious tradition. No geographical frontiers help it to arrive at a common consciousness and it has no sense of a common history, as nations have, except the minimal common experience of a war partnership through which a terrible foe was defeated. But the very defeat of the foe removes one factor of cohesion.

For this reason our civilization will probably require ages before it will master the problem of our common life on the world level. The inevitability of a considerable degree of frustration in achieving what we must achieve is one aspect of our existence for which our culture has not prepared us.

If technics in modern communications have created a potential world-community, which finds difficulty in becoming actual, technics in production have shattered old forms of justice and made the achievement of new ones difficult. The modern machine becomes larger and larger as it becomes more and more efficient. It long since has divorced the skill of the worker from his tool. It has to a certain degree divorced the worker from his skill, which is now increasingly in the machine. It has thus made the worker powerless, except insofar as common organized action has given him a degree of social and political power. It has on the other hand constantly increased the power of fewer and fewer centers of economic authority. It may be regarded as an axiom of political justice that disproportions of powers increase the hazard to justice; for to be armed with power means that the temptation to do what one wants increases. And what one wants immediately is usually not the common welfare.

The cultural inadequacies of our age have contributed to the difficulties we face in achieving economic justice. For our age began with the presupposition, derived from a naturalistic philosophy, that economic justice would be achieved by a natural equilibrium of social and economic forces. The eighteenth-century physiocrats, and Adam Smith after them, made the mistake of assuming that history, like nature, has limited potencies. Actually the very character of human history is to give the forces of nature unlimited scope. The "pre-established harmony of nature," which eighteenth-century enlightenment thought would guarantee justice, has actually never existed in history, though there were some evidences of it in an agrarian and in an early commercial age. But an industrial age disturbed all these harmonies and created monopolistic power in a realm where a harmony of powers was to reign. One of the most ironic facts of history is that Adam Smith elaborated his theory, upon which modern capitalism is based, at the precise moment when the steam engine was invented.

We in America suffer particularly from the legacy of the eighteenth-century naturalistic determinism. We have developed technics more fully than any nation. Yet every effort to achieve social justice within terms set by modern productive arrangements is dogged by nostalgic social and economic theories which have no relevance to our actual problems. The Marxist answer to this problem may be wrong; it is certainly not wholly correct. Yet it recognizes some aspects of the problem which liberalism does not.

Modern society has already proved that long before it will allow the process of centralization of economic power to work itself out to the catastrophic conclusion which Marxism predicted and expected, it will take political measures to arrest the tendency toward irresponsible and disproportionate economic power. Democracy is not quite as potent an instrument as the eighteenth century believed; but it is more potent than the Marxists imagined. The poor are armed with political power in a democracy. They use that political power to redress the balances in the economic sphere. Whether the power is sufficient to achieve a true balance is another question. It may not be. It may be that oligarchies of the economically powerful may possess sufficient strength to destroy the political instruments in the hands of their foes before those political instruments finally destroy their privileged position in society. This is the meaning of fascism in the field of domestic relations. It may be that the consequences of fascism, where it was tried, have been sufficiently horrible to prevent a drift toward that answer. But we cannot be sure.

At any rate the achievement of a decent minimum of economic security for the masses in our civilization is still an unsolved problem. It may not be as stubborn a problem as the international one, though there are some who regard it as more stubborn. There are nations like Britain and Sweden who have moved far enough toward its solution to encourage the hope that they will continue to approach the goal of economic justice without running the risk of social catastrophe. It is not certain that we are as safe against social catastrophe in this country. Our working people are less politically mature than some of the workers of other nations. And the possessors of economic power in America are on the whole remarkably stupid. Even now they would have us believe that the intricate task of shifting from a war to a peace economy can be accomplished merely by relaxing governmental restraints upon the economic and industrial process and allowing everything to find its own level. Catastrophe lies in that direction. We shall probably be too wise to follow the road to that catastrophe consistently; but we are hardly wise enough to avoid tentative efforts to restore an unmanaged unity and harmony of economic process.

Even if we avoid the most obvious mistakes we cannot find a simple solution to the problem of economic justice which confronts us. Russia has revealed that it is possible to pay too high a price in freedom for the economic security of the masses. The consistent socialization of all economic power is no more adequate a solution for our problem than a consistent disavowal of political authority upon economic process. The latter leads to anarchy as the former leads to tyranny. The wisest nations experiment in order to find a middle way which will insure a maximum of freedom and security. That middle way certainly involves the socialization of some forms of property that cannot otherwise be brought under social control. It means placing certain governmental checks upon other forms of economic activity and yet allowing freedom in the economic process wherever possible, which means wherever that freedom will not tend to destroy freedom.

The cultural weaknesses which have contributed to our crisis, and which make it difficult for us to fully understand the depth and breadth of it, are in some cases immediately related to the political and economic crisis and in other cases they have a more indirect relationship.

The most obvious cultural presupposition that is in immediate relation to the crisis is the excessive individualism of the culture of the seventeenth and eighteenth centuries. This individualism resulted from the breaking of the medieval organic forms of social life and from the natural illusions of the rising bourgeois class. Having new and dynamic forms of social power, they regarded the individual as much more self-sufficient than he really is. The bourgeois class emphasized the ideal of liberty to the point of imperiling the community and obscuring social responsibility. They elaborated social theories according to which human societies are created when atomic individuals come together by a "social contract"—that is, through a pure fiat of the human will. Actually, no decision in human society is ever taken that does not presuppose some form of community previous to the decision; for society is as primordial as the individual.

The excessive individualism of the bourgeois classes led to a collectivist reaction on the part of the working classes. This collectivism of Marxism is probably closer to the truth than bourgeois individualism; but it is also in error when it assumes that a frictionless harmony between the individual and the community can be established. In reality the individual has a form of constitutional spiritual freedom which makes it inevitable that even the best community will frustrate as well as fulfill the highest aspirations of the human spirit. Love is the law of life for the individual, in the sense that no human being can fulfil himself within himself. He is fulfilled only in the community. But the same individual rises in indeterminate degree beyond all communal and social relevancies. It is this transcendent freedom of the individual which is guarded and expressed in the historic religions of the West, Jewish and Christian. Modern culture disavowed these traditional religions. In consequence it emphasized freedom in society to the point of destroying society; and in reaction emphasized social solidarity to the point of imperiling the dignity of the individual.

The class warfare between the bourgeois and the working classes which contributed so much to the undoing of European nations was not merely a political and economic conflict. It was also a cultural and religious conflict, in the sense that two forms of secularized religion were embattled. The one religion made the individual self-sufficient to the point of making man the idolatrous end of his own existence. The other religion made society the idolatrous end of the existence of the individual. This is a conflict which cannot be resolved within the presuppositions of a culture that fails to measure the character of man's historic existence in its full depth. For a man is a historical creature, constantly fulfilling his life by realizing higher forms of communal life and yet always standing beyond even the widest social obligations and realizations in the highest reaches of his spiritual freedom.

The analysis of the excessive individualism and collectivism of a secular culture has thus already brought us to another aspect of our cultural crisis. The "naturalism" of our culture was celebrated as a great spiritual achievement in the heyday of our era. It was supposed to prevent men from being beguiled by false eternities. They would realize the highest historic possibilities the more certainly if they were no longer led astray by illusions of eternal salvation and redemption. Actually there have been many forms of religious "other-worldliness" which were merely compensations for frustrations, and expressions of social defeatism. It was good that men should be emancipated from them. There are also forms of religious "super-naturalism" which conceive the world as a kind of layer-cake affair, with two layers, the one natural and the other supernatural, the one physical and the other "spiritual." There is only one world; just as man in the unity of his physical and spiritual life is one. Religious dualism is an error. But so is a naturalistic monism that seeks to comprehend the full dimension of human existence from the standpoint of man's relation to nature.

Man is undoubtedly a creature of nature, subject to its necessities and limitations. But an excessive emphasis upon this aspect of man's existence obscures the full dimension of human personality. It is by man's freedom over natural process and limitation that he is able to make history. But the same freedom which lies at the basis of man's historic creativity is also the root of human evil. Thus man, whose nature it is to be realized beyond himself in the life of his fellows, is also able to corrupt the community and make it the tool of his interests. The possibilities of evil as well as of good are much greater than modern culture assumed.

The naturalistic assumptions of modern culture prompted the belief that history was an extension of the evolutionary process of nature, that this evolutionary process guaranteed a higher and higher achievement of the good, however that good might be defined. It was frequently defined in contradictory terms.

But human freedom breaks the limits of nature, upsetting its limited harmonies and giving a demonic dimension to its conflicts. There is therefore progress in human history; but it is a progress of all human potencies, both for good and for evil. A culture which imagined that history was moving naturally to a wider and more inclusive community, toward the "parliament of mankind and the federation of the world," was naturally completely overtaken by the catastrophe of our era. It was not prepared for the tragic character of human history. It did not anticipate that a potential world-community would announce itself to history in global wars. After the First World War the natural attitude of modern culture was to regard the war as a capricious interruption of the stream of progress, occasioned by an evil nation. Even the second world catastrophe was sometimes interpreted in such terms.

The historical optimism of our culture was thus derived from a view of man and history that failed to measure the full dimension of the human spirit and of its historic achievements. Man is able by the technical elaboration of his powers to establish a wider and wider community. But the same skills also arm him with a mighty weapon of individual and collective egotism when he desires to set himself against the community.

While it is quite possible that we will finally discover the right political instruments for ordering the communal life upon a world scale, certain aspects of this task are not fully comprehended in our culture. The difficulty, for one thing, is not fully understood. It is not understood that the same technics that integrate the world community also arm the individual nations and encourage them to follow their own respective courses and possibly to threaten the world-community with anarchy. Because the struggle between the universal and the particular, between egotism and the community, is a more stubborn struggle on every level, the whole of human history is more tragic than modern culture had assumed;

and it will continue to be more tragic because the sources of conflict do not lie in the past. They reappear in every historical level.

Nor is it fully understood that there are no absolute securities and stabilities in human history; and there will be rather fewer in the future than in the past. Modern culture is inveterately utopian and is always looking for a security in the future that men did not have in the past. It believes, for instance, that the failure to master nature made man insecure in the past and that modern technics have overcome this insecurity. Actually the same technics by which we gain security in nature increase our insecurity in human history and in the ever larger communities in which we must live.

Smaller communities are always close to nature, held together by a natural force of consanguinity and supported by nature's abundance. Large communities are held together by the artifice of statesmen and supplied by intricate arrangements of commerce and communication. They depend upon the human will and imagination, which frequently fail.

There is thus a complete misinterpretation of the future. The future may be filled with glorious achievements, but not with greater securities than in the past. This means that a culture which failed to understand that human life cannot be completely fulfilled in human history will be inadequate for man in the future, as it becomes more fully recognized that human life is subject to historical frustration even on the highest level of historical achievement. This does not validate crude forms of "other-worldliness." But it will make relevant once more the real meaning of the transcendental reference in historical religions.

Finally it must become apparent that no matter how effective the social instruments for the protection of communal order are, they are never adequate without an inner moral and religious check. The older religions frequently made the mistake of placing all emphasis upon moral discipline and neglecting the various forms of social and political restraint by which justice is achieved. That is why democracy was frequently the fruit of a secular culture, though this is not altogether the case since the presuppositions of democracy are deeply imbedded in Hebraic prophetism and Christian faith. Today it is frequently assumed that the right kind of economic organization and the right kind of political order will guarantee the virtue of man and the welfare of society.

Marxism assumes that a wrong economic organization is the root of all human evil and that on the other side of a revolution men will be virtuous and human ambitions will be perfectly related to common welfare. Liberalism is not quite so naive but frequently looks upon democratic political forms as the guarantors of virtue. Actually, the freedom of man is such that no perfection of social instruments obviates the necessities of inner moral checks upon human ambitions. On the other hand, it must be observed, of course, that inner checks are also not sufficient if we do not achieve the best possible social instruments for checking self-will and egotism and for increasing the common and mutual concerns of men.

There is thus no reason to suggest that the regeneration of the world depends merely upon a religious and moral revival which will create the "good" men of old without whom no social system can function. Good men with social and political instruments inadequate to the new dimensions of a social problem are futile. But on the other hand, all purely social or political interpretations of the human problem are unavailing. Man is more social than bourgeois liberalism assumed. His final freedom reaches beyond all social responsibilities and communal fulfillments in a way that modern forms of collectivism do not understand. There are dimensions of his existence which are fully understood in the historic religions. They recognize that his moral freedom and responsibility have no limit or end except in God. But the historic religions were on the whole oblivious to the dynamic character of human history, particularly as it has unfolded since the introduction of technics. The Hebrew prophets did indeed have a conception of a dynamic history moving toward a great fulfillment. But neither the Jewish nor the Christian faith have ever done full justice to this aspect of prophetism.

It remained for modern culture to interpret the dynamic character of history; but it did so too optimistically and without a full awareness of the depth of evil and the height of creativity which might be unfolded in history. This blindness to the depth of good and evil was derived from the mistake of measuring the whole human enterprise in too shallow a dimension.

There is, therefore, no possibility of fully understanding the tragic character of the history through which we are passing, or of living sanely in a period of great frustration as well as of great historical achievement, or of placing inner moral checks upon the dynamism of man, without the resources of an older religious culture. Our modern culture is too flat, too lacking in the tragic sense of life, and too blind to the total dimension of existence to be an adequate guide for our day.

Yet our problem is not solved by some simple "return to religion," as the traditional religionists would have it. An adequate culture must combine the modern sense of historical dynamism with historic religion's sense of the dimension of life that transcends history.

The last great cultural and political crisis of Western history involved the breakdown of a medieval culture and a feudal civilization. The one was destroyed by the dynamism of a scientific culture and the other by the power of a rising bourgeois civilization. Both this scientific culture and this bourgeois civilization have now reached the period of disintegration. The facts of life are too complex and too tragic to be comprehended within the limits of a secular culture; and the disharmonies, worldwide social maladjustments and worldwide communal issues are too stubborn to be solved by the social instruments, either individualistic or collectivistic, which our modern civilization uses today.

An adequate culture for our day must therefore combine the historical dynamism of our culture with the depth of the culture of previous ages.

Two Forms of Utopianism

[*Christianity and Society*, Vol. 12 (Autumn 1947), pp. 6–7.]

THERE is a curious pathos in the conflict between the Western and the Russian world. The Western world, though partly Christian, is primarily informed by the secular religion of faith in progress. The Russian world is animated by the secular creed of faith in redemption through revolution. The conflict is of course something more than an ideological one. It is a conflict, or at least tension, between two great centers of power, which might mistrust each other even if they had no ideological chasm between them.

But insofar as the conflict is ideological, each side is involved in a situation for which its creed offers no source of understanding. The liberal creed of progress assumes that men are progressing toward higher and higher forms of social life and more and more inclusive loyalties. The Nazi rebellion against a world community was difficult to explain in terms of this faith and was usually put down as a mysterious reversion to barbarism, which would not finally impede the onward march of humanity toward world community. Now the liberal world is confronted not by a cynical, but by a utopian foe, who also believes in world community, not by evolution but by revolution.

The Russians on the other hand believe that the capitalist world, though sworn to enmity against communism, will finally be vanquished because capitalism is subject to successive crises which will undermine its strength and make it ripe for conquest. The stubbornness with which the Russians resist, and refuse to come to terms with, a technically superior foe can only be explained by their hope that this foe will finally be weakened by economic crises and become more manageable. One of the primary perils of war actually consists in the possibility that Russia may underestimate the residual health of a capitalist society and challenge it, despite its technical superiority, in the hope that what the Communists call the "inner contradictions" of capitalism will assure the victory of communism.

In other words two secular religions of world redemption are in conflict with one another. One cannot deny that there is a special pathos in a conflict in the world community between two political forces each of which underestimates the complexities of history and is blind to the truth which the other side holds, and both of which fail to understand the tragic character of human history. The Communist creed of world redemption is the more dangerous because it is informed by a hard utopianism, while the liberal world is informed by soft utopianism. Hard utopianism might be defined as the creed of those who claim to embody the perfect community and who therefore feel themselves morally justified in using every instrument of guile or force against those who oppose their assumed perfection. Soft utopianism is the creed of those who do not claim to embody perfection, but expect perfection to emerge out of the ongoing process of history. The soft utopians are obviously not as dangerous and fanatic as the hard utopians; but they are at a disadvantage in their conflict with the hard utopians because they do not understand that history makes the problems of man's togetherness more, rather than less, complex. Many of them are still dreaming of creating an ideal world government without answering the question how we could beguile the Russians to accept its authority, or for that matter, how it could get past the United States Senate.

Meanwhile we permit political realism to be monopolized by our generals, who recognize that we are involved in a power struggle and assume that we are involved in nothing else. By seeking to protect the Western world merely through superior power, they aggravate the mistrust between Russia and the West. Our idealists lack the realism which recognizes the immediate perils of our existence. And our realists are completely blind to the more ultimate dimensions of the tragic conflict in which we are involved. The Russian realism, on the other hand, is informed by the kind of dogmatism which underestimates both the genuine desire for peace in the Western world and also the residual political health of the democratic nations.

In such a situation no peace can be guaranteed; but war is not inevitable. The Christian faith could achieve a new relevance to our immediate issues if it should help to open the eyes of both hard and soft utopians. There is small prospect, in fact, of the Christian faith leavening the lump of hard utopianism. But it is still a force, though a minor one, in the democratic world. In that world it might persuade us to recognize the tragic character of the vicious circle of mistrust in which two schemes of world redemption are involved. It might prompt us to combine with our loyalty to our own ideals of a democratic civilization some sense of an overarching common human predicament in which both Communists and democrats are involved. It might thus assuage our fears and hatreds against communism without relaxing our immediate defenses against its immediate perils, but also without placing our whole reliance on such defenses. It might finally prompt us to achieve a measure of serenity even in an era in which it has become apparent that no complete security against atomic destruction can be achieved. For one of the greatest perils for both the Russians and ourselves lies in the hidden and unacknowledged fears of catastrophe which prompt us to hysteria.

It is not that we refuse to acknowledge the actual peril of atomic destruction. We refuse to admit the more general problem arising from the fact that all human life is insecure and that the power of modern man has aggravated and not mitigated this general insecurity. Faith does not of itself solve any particular political issue. But a genuine faith which transcends all vicissitudes of nature and history enables men to live with the kind of courage which must enter into all particular solutions.

Christian Faith and Political Controversy

[*Christianity and Crisis*, Vol. 12 (July 21, 1952), pp. 87–88.]

A PRESIDENTIAL election year once again brings into focus the problem of how Christians should relate their religious commitments to their political opinions and decisions. This is a problem of conscience for every individual Christian. It is also a practical problem for Christian congregations and communities. It arises as a problem for the church because the church is a community of faith which is not organized on the basis of common political convictions; yet its members do have political convictions and sometimes very contradictory ones. The more passionately they are held, the more they rise to the religious level and the more they tend to affront fellow Christians who hold different convictions. Sometimes the problem emerges, particularly with reference to different convictions between pastors and congregations. For, generally speaking, the congregations of American Protestantism are more conservative politically than their clerical leaders.

We can approach a solution of the problem of relating religious commitments to political decisions by excluding two wrong answers to the issue. The one wrong answer is to equate religious and political commitments and to regard every political decision as simply derived from our faith. This is a wrong answer because political issues deal with complex problems of justice, every solution for which contains morally ambiguous elements. All political positions are morally ambiguous because, in the realm of politics and economics, self-interest and power must be harnessed and beguiled rather than eliminated. In other words, forces which are morally dangerous must be used despite their peril. Politics always aims at some kind of a harmony or balance of interest, and such a harmony cannot be regarded as directly related to the final harmony of love of the Kingdom of God. All men are naturally inclined to obscure the morally ambiguous element in their political cause by investing it with religious sanctity. This is why religion is more frequently a source of confusion than of light in the political realm. The tendency to equate our political with our Christian convictions causes politics to generate idolatry.

The other wrong answer stands at the opposite extreme. It is to find no relevance at all between our faith and our political actions. This answer is wrong because it denies the seriousness of our political decisions and obscures our Christian responsibilities for the good order and justice of our civil community.

If we rule out these two extremes, we still face the primary question of how politics is to be related to faith. We can advance a little farther toward a solution of the problem if we recognize that political issues represent various grades and levels which range all the way from clear moral issues to problems of strategy and means.

It is obvious, for instance, that the Christian churches of America have, with a fair degree of consistency, espoused the idea of America's responsibility to a world community, and have resisted nationalist and isolationist politics in the name of the Christian faith. They have been right in doing so. But this broad moral purpose must be distinguished from problems of strategy. Various strategic devices will be advanced as the best ways of fulfilling our responsibilities. Such devices can never be invested with full religious sanctity. It would be impossible to claim, for instance, that the Christian faith requires that America give preference to either the European or the Asiatic field of strategy, or that we should defend the free world primarily by air, rather than by land, power.

In the same fashion the commandment "Thou shalt love thy neighbor as thyself" brings us under religious and moral compulsions to eliminate the violations of brotherhood in the field of race relations. But it can hardly compel us to choose between the efficacy of a state as against a Federal Fair Employment Practices Act. In such questions of strategy there are reasons for honest differences of opinion.

In actual life, however, no clear distinction between moral principles and strategy can be made. This is why Christian convictions that deal only with ultimate principle and exclude strategic issues tend to become wholly irrelevant. Yet the farther one moves from a principle that is clearly related to the love commandment to detailed applications in particular situations, the more hazardous the decision becomes, and the more impossible it is to compel others to a similar conviction by appeal to a common faith.

That is why it is important to distinguish between the responsibility of individual Christians and voluntary groups, and the responsibility of the church as a community of faith. Christians must make these hazardous political decisions with full recognition that others equally devoted to the common good may arrive at contrary conclusions. They will be less affronted and baffled by the different conclusions if they have some humble recognition of the taint of individual and collective self-interest which colors even our purest political and moral ideals. The different emphases, for instance, that the more and the less privileged members of a democratic community give to the value of freedom on the one hand and to the value of justice on the other (a difference that is at the very heart of politics in all free societies) should be recognized as flowing inevitably from the peculiar interests and ideologies of each group.

We are well aware that unity in a free society requires a high degree of what our secular friends define as tolerance. As Christians we are inclined to regard the attitude of tolerance as rooted in a religious humility, which recognizes the partial and fragmentary character of all human wisdom and the interested character of all human striving. Whenever religion obscures, rather than illumines, this human situation, it tends to aggravate political controversies and adds an element of pretension to the natural self-righteousness of men. On the other hand, a mere emphasis upon religious humility may empty the political struggle of seriousness by persuading men that all their causes are equally true or equally false. That is why it is important to emphasize our responsibility for hazardous political decisions at the same time that we seek to understand the reasons why different men of equal sincerity and wisdom arrive at contrary conclusions. We must not obscure the issue of justice which is hidden in every political question or pretend to be gods and not men, transcending the frailties of mortals. Ideally a democratic society is best preserved by a religious quality of life which regards our political as our other decisions of great importance, even while recognizing the incapacity of men to arrive at a purely rational, or purely moral, or purely Christian solution of any perplexing problem.

Fragments

ON WORKING FOR A MORE JUST AND PEACEFUL WORLD

We can work for a better world order, a more stable peace and more just relations among the nations, without the illusion that it is possible to create a perfectly safe and perpetual peace. This hope is also an illusion because nothing is absolutely safe in history. The illusion produces despair because the insecurity of history always reveals itself in the end—if not in our generation, then in the generation of our children. Man has no final security except in the sovereignty and majesty of God who presides over history and can make man's wrath to praise him.

"Religion and Modern Knowledge," in *Man's Destiny in Eternity*, ed. A. H. Compton (Boston: Beacon Press, 1949), p. 135.

ON A NATION'S CONSCIENCE AND ITS LAWS

If a nation loses its moral substance, no laws can save it. For laws do not create but merely formulate what the conscience of a people contains.

"Honesty in America," *The Messenger*, Vol. 16 (July 31, 1951), p. 7.

ON RELIGION AND POLITICS

The fact is that a simple identification of religious and political convictions, whether on the right or the left, is noxious. The evils of religious politics of any shade are due to the fact that religion deals with life's ultimate needs and meanings, while politics must inevitably strive for proximate ends of life and must use ambiguous means to attain them. Therefore, it is dangerous to claim the sanctity of the ultimate for political ends and means. It may be very important to win a particular election; but no conflict between political parties is ever a clear contest between right and wrong. Some contests, as for instance the struggle against tyranny, may be quite unequivocal in moral meaning. But generally the moral ambiguity in political struggles is very considerable. . . .

Therefore, the test of a creative relation between our religious life and our political action is a double one. On the one hand, the question is whether the life of faith prompts us to participate responsibly in the struggle for greater justice.

The other question is whether our faith prompts us to discriminate, rather than indiscriminate, partisanship. For true faith must generate discrimination. The worship of the true God, rather than the gods of our own image, must make us aware of the mixture of motives in our own striving and the residual truth in the position of the competitor or foe. The mark of "bad" religion is always fanaticism, whether on the right or the left. The mark of true religion is always a measure of charity and forgiveness even in the stoutest championship of the proximate ends of justice.

"Religious Politics," *Christianity and Society*, Vol. 16 (Autumn 1951), pp. 4–5.

ON BURKE, MADISON, AND THE FRENCH ENLIGHTENMENT

The French Enlightenment . . . had a total philosophy of life based on confidence in the perfectibility of man and on the idea of historical progress. These two ideas were basic to all the political miscalculations of the Enlightenment and were the source of its errors. "Liberalism" acquired a special connotation as a philosophy of life which did not take the factors of interest and power seriously, which expected all parochial loyalties to be dissolved in more universal loyalties; and which was indifferent to organically and historically established loyalties and rights under the illusion that it would be simple for rational man to devise more ideal communities and rights. The liberalism of the French Enlightenment was thus based upon illusions as to the nature of man and of history. . . . These were the illusions which Burke challenged in *Reflections on the Revolution in France.* The philosophy of the Enlightenment was not shared by such conservatives as John Adams or such Jeffersonians as James Madison. Our Constitution was, in fact, informed by a realism which contradicted all the illusions of the Enlightenment.

"Liberalism: Illusions and Realities," *The New Republic*, Vol. 133 (July 4, 1955), pp. 12–13.

ON LOVE AND JUSTICE

Love as a substitute for justice is odious, but love as a supplement to justice is an absolute necessity.

"The Gospel in Future America," *The Christian Century*, Vol. 75 (June 18, 1958), p. 714.

ON VIRTUES OF AN OPEN SOCIETY

The ultimate virtue of an open society is not merely the political system of self-government, a government "of the people, by the people, and for the people," though that is its immediate virtue. The political virtue of a free society is that it makes power responsible, disperses power into as many centers as possible, thereby creating a system of checks and balances, and refuses immunity from criticism and review to any center of power and prestige. The more ultimate virtue of an open society is that it does not coerce either the community or the total process of history into a dogmatic mold. History flows through the alternations of government in an open society, taking courses that not even the most prescient leaders of the political party conflict could have foreseen. This is its ultimate virtue because this characteristic of an open society conforms to the nature of man as both creature and creator of history.

"The Unintended Virtues of an Open Society," *Christianity and Crisis*, Vol. 21 (July 24, 1961), p.132.

ON THE PERIL TO CULTURE IN A TECHNICAL SOCIETY

The peril of vulgarization of our culture through preoccupation with the means, rather than the goals, of life . . . is obvious on every hand. We face the peril of the humane and human substance of our culture, and of the whole human enterprise, being subordinated to the immediate ends of physical abundance through technical competence.

"The Present Heritage of the Long Encounter between Christian Faith and Western Civilization," *Harvard Divinity School Bulletin*, Vol. 26 (October 1961), p. 10.

PART III
EVENTS AND ISSUES

The War Situation

[*Christianity and Society,* Vol. 6 (Winter 1940–41), pp. 3–4.] While Britain stood alone against the Nazi peril early in World War II, Niebuhr wrote this piece. Soon thereafter America began aiding the British through Lend-Lease.

AFTER the scare of last June, when it seemed for a few moments as if the whole of Europe would fall under the Nazi heel with the collapse of France, the American people have gradually come to the conclusion that Britain must be supported at all costs. The heroic resistance of the British people has given us time to come to our senses, survey the meaning of a possible German victory, organize our production with the purpose of increasing our material support of the British cause and consolidate the will of the nation behind something like a general, though not quite unanimous, purpose.

Though we have moved rapidly, it now appears that we have not moved rapidly enough, either in defining our purpose or in carrying it out. The fact is that Britain is in the gravest peril. We know the stuff of which this nation is made well enough to know that there will be no sudden collapse. However, the ability of the Germans to continue night bombing on city after city and the increasing toll taken by submarine and bomber of the British merchant fleet warrants anxiety with regard to the future. . . . It is obvious that we will have to increase our aid measurably, if Britain is to carry the burden of this battle.

Whether we go beyond the present generally accepted policy of all possible material aid to Britain, and add credits and beyond that shipping, and beyond that not yet devised forms of support and even in the final instance, belligerent aid, is a question which this journal regards as matters of policy and not of principle. The political principle upon which we are agreed is that everything must be done that can be done to insure the defeat of the Nazis. The moral viewpoint which makes such a conviction possible is that enslavement to tyranny is worse than war.

The Christian Faith and the World Crisis

[*Christianity and Crisis,* Vol. 1 (February 10, 1941), pp. 4–6.] This was Niebuhr's first article in *Christianity and Crisis,* founded to counter American isolationism and pacifism in the face of the Nazi menace to Western civilization.

IT is our purpose to devote this modest journal to an exposition of our Christian faith in its relation to world events. This first article will seek, therefore, to offer a general introduction to the faith that is in us. We believe that many current interpretations have obscured important elements in that faith and have thereby confused the Christian conscience. This confusion has been brought into sharp relief by the world crisis; but it existed before the crisis, and it may well continue after the crisis is over. We therefore regard our task as one that transcends the urgent problems of the hour, though we do not deny that these problems are the immediate occasion for our enterprise.

At the present moment a basic difference of conviction with regard to what Christianity is and what it demands runs through the whole of American Protestantism and cuts across all the traditional denominational distinctions. There is, on the one hand, a school of Christian thought that believes war could be eliminated if only Christians and other men of good will refused resolutely enough to have anything to do with conflict. Another school of thought, while conceding that war is one of the most vivid revelations of sin in human history, does not find the disavowal of war so simple a matter. The proponents of the latter position believe that there are historic situations in which refusal to defend the inheritance of a civilization, however imperfect, against tyranny and aggression may result in consequences even worse than war.

This journal intends to express and, if possible, to clarify this second viewpoint. We do not believe that the Christian faith as expressed in the New Testament and as interpreted in historic Christianity, both Catholic and Protestant, implies the confidence that evil and injustice in history can be overcome by such simple methods as are currently equated with Christianity. We believe that modern Christian perfectionism is tinctured with utopianism derived from a secular culture. In our opinion this utopianism contributed to the tardiness of the democracies in defending themselves against the perils of a new barbarism, and (in America at least) it is easily compounded with an irresponsible and selfish nationalism.

We intend this journal to be both polemic and irenic, as far as human frailty will permit the combination of these two qualities. It will be polemic in the sense that we shall combat what seem to us false interpretations of our faith, and consequent false analyses of our world and of our duties in it. It will be irenic in the sense that we shall seek to appreciate the extent to which perfectionist and pacifist interpretations of Christianity are derived from genuine and important elements in our common faith.

Perfectionists are right in their conviction that our civilization stands under the judgment of God; no one can have an easy conscience about the social and political anarchy out of which the horrible tyranny that now threatens us arose. But they are wrong in assuming that we have no right or duty to defend a civilization, despite its imperfections, against worse alternatives. They are right in insisting that love is the ultimate law of life. But they have failed to realize to what degree the sinfulness of all men, even the best, makes justice between competing interests and conflicting wills a perennial necessity of history.

The perfectionists rightly recognize that it may be very noble for an individual to sacrifice his life or interests rather than participate in the claims and counterclaims of the struggle for justice (of which war may always be the *ultima ratio*). They are wrong in making no distinction between an individual act of self-abnegation and a political policy of submission to injustice, whereby lives and interests other than our own are defrauded or destroyed. They seek erroneously to build a political platform upon individual perfection. Medieval perfectionism, whatever its limitations, wisely avoided these errors. It excluded even the family from the possible consequences of an individual's absolute ethic, and it was profoundly aware of the impossibility of making its rigorous standards universal.

We believe that there are many Christians whose moral inclinations might persuade them to take the same view of current problems as our own, except for the fact that they are inhibited by religious presuppositions that they regard as more "purely" Christian than those represented by the consensus of the Church through all the ages. Therefore we will begin with an analysis of these religious presuppositions.

Christians are agreed that the God who is revealed in Christ is source and end of our existence and that therefore his character and will are the norm and standard of our conduct. It is only in recent decades, however, that it has been believed that the "gentleness" of Jesus was a sufficient and final revelation of the character of God, that this character was one of pure love and mercy, and that this revelation stood in contradiction to an alleged portrayal of a God of wrath in the Old Testament.

Both the Old and the New Testament take the wrath of God as well as the mercy of God seriously. The divine mercy, apprehended by Christian faith in the life and death of Christ, is not some simple kindness indifferent to good and evil. The whole point of the Christian doctrine of Atonement is that God cannot be merciful without fulfilling within himself, and on man's behalf, the requirements of divine justice. However difficult it may be to give a fully rational account of what Christ's atoning death upon the Cross means to Christian faith, this mystery, never fully comprehended by and yet not wholly incomprehensible to faith, speaks to us of a mercy that transcends but also satisfies the demands of justice.

The biblical answer to the problem of evil in human history is a radical answer, precisely because human evil is recognized as a much more stubborn fact than is realized in some modern versions of the Christian faith. These versions do not take the problem of justice in history seriously, because they have obscured what the Bible has to say about the relation of justice to mercy in the very heart of God. Every sensitive Christian must feel a sense of unworthiness when he is compelled by historic destiny to act as an instrument of God's justice. Recognition of the common guilt that makes him and his enemy kin must persuade him to imitate the mercy of God, even while he seeks to fulfill the demands of justice. But he will seek to elude such responsibilities only if he believes, as many modern Christians do, that he might, if he tried a little harder, achieve an individual or collective vantage point of guiltlessness from which to proceed against evil doers. There is no such vantage point.

Christians are agreed that Christ must be the norm of our human life as well as the revelation of the character of God. But many modern versions of Christianity have forgotten to what degree the perfect love of Christ was recognized both in the Bible and in the Christian ages as finally transcending all historic possibilities. The same St. Paul who admonishes us to grow into the stature of Christ insists again and again that we are "saved by faith" and not "by works"; which is to say that our final peace is not the moral peace of having become what Christ defines as our true nature but is the religious peace of knowing that a divine mercy accepts our loyalty to Christ despite our continued betrayal of him.

It cannot be denied that these emphases are full of pitfalls for the faithful. On the one side there is always the possibility that we will not take Christ as our norm seriously enough, and that we will rest prematurely in the divine mercy. On the other hand an abstract perfectionism is tempted to obscure the most obvious facts about human nature and to fall into the fury of self-righteousness. The Protestant Reformation was in part a protest against what seemed to the Reformers an overly optimistic Catholic doctrine of human perfection through the infusion of divine grace. Yet modern Protestant interpretations of the same issue make the Catholic doctrine wise and prudent by comparison.

Once it is recognized that the stubbornness of human selfishness makes the achievement of justice in human society no easy matter, it ought to be possible to see that war is but a vivid revelation of certain perennial aspects of human history. Life is never related to life in terms of a perfect and loving conformity of will with will. Where there is sin and selfishness there must also be a struggle for justice; and this justice is always partially an achievement of our love for the other and partially a result of our yielding to his demands and pressures. The intermediate norm of justice is particularly important in the institutional and collective relationships of mankind. But even in individual and personal relations the ultimate level of sacrificial self-giving is not reached without an intermediate level of justice. On this level the first consideration is not that life should be related to life through the disinterested concern of each for the other, but that life should be prevented from exploiting, enslaving or taking advantage of other life. Sometimes this struggle takes very tragic forms.

It is important for Christians to remember that every structure of justice, as embodied in political and economic institutions, (a) contains elements of injustice that stand in contradiction to the law of love; (b) contains higher possibilities of justice that must be realized in terms of institutions and structures; and (c) that it must be supplemented by the graces of individual and personal generosity and mercy. Yet when the mind is not confused by utopian illusions it is not difficult to recognize genuine achievements of justice and to feel under obligation to defend them against the threats of tyranny and the negation of justice.

Love must be regarded as the final flower and fruit of justice. When it is substituted for justice it degenerates into sentimentality and may become the accomplice of tyranny.

Looking at the tragic contemporary scene within this frame of reference, we feel that American Christianity is all too prone to disavow its responsibilities for the preservation of our civilization against the perils of totalitarian aggression. We are well aware of the sins of all the nations, including our own, which have contributed to the chaos of our era. We know to what degree totalitarianism represents false answers to our own unsolved problems—political, economic, spiritual.

Yet we believe the task of defending the rich inheritance of our civilization to be an imperative one, however much we might desire that our social system were more worthy of defense. We believe that the possibility of correcting its faults and extending its gains may be annulled for centuries if this external peril is not resolutely faced. We do not find it particularly impressive to celebrate one's sensitive conscience by enlarging upon all the well-known evils of our western world and equating them with the evils of the totalitarian systems. It is just as important for Christians to be discriminating in their judgments, as for them to recognize the element of sin in all human endeavors. We think it dangerous to allow religious sensitivity to obscure the fact that Nazi tyranny intends to annihilate the Jewish race, to subject the nations of Europe to the dominion of a "master" race, to extirpate the Christian religion, to annul the liberties and legal standards that are the priceless heritage of ages of Christian and humanistic culture, to make truth the prostitute of political power, to seek world dominion through its satraps and allies, and generally to destroy the very fabric of our western civilization.

Our own national tardiness in becoming fully alive to this peril has been compounded of national selfishness and religious confusion. In recent months American opinion has begun to respond to the actualities of the situation and to sense the fateful destiny that unites us with all free peoples, whether momentarily overrun by the aggressor or still offering heroic resistance. How far our assistance is to be carried is a matter of policy and strategy. It could be a matter of principle only if it were conceded that an absolute line could be drawn in terms of Christian principle between "measures short of war" and war itself. But those who think such a line can be drawn have nevertheless opposed measures short of war. They rightly have pointed out that such measures cannot be guaranteed against the risk of total involvement.

The measures now being taken for the support of the democracies are a logical expression of the unique conditions of America's relation to the world. They do justice on the one hand to our responsibilities for a common civilization that transcends the hemispheres, and on the other hand to the fact that we are not as immediately imperiled as other nations. Whether our freedom from immediate peril will enable us to persevere in the reservations that we still maintain cannot be decided in the abstract. The exigencies of the future must determine the issue.

We cannot, of course, be certain that defeat of the Nazis will usher in a new order of international justice in Europe and the world. We do know what a Nazi victory would mean, and our first task must therefore be to prevent it. Yet it cannot be our only task, for the problem of organizing the technical civilization of the western world upon a new basis of economic and international justice, so that the anarchy and decay that have characterized our life in the past three decades will be arrested and our technical capacities will be made fruitful rather than suicidal, is one which must engage our best resources. We must give some thought and attention to this great issue even while we are forced to ward off a horrible alternative.

We believe that the Christian faith can and must make its own contribution to this issue. The task of building a new world, as well as the tragic duty of saving the present world from tyranny, will require resources of understanding and resolution which are inherent in the Christian faith. The profoundest insights of the Christian faith cannot be expressed by the simple counsel that men ought to be more loving, and that if they became so the problems of war and of international organization would solve themselves.

Yet there are times when hopes for the future, as well as contrition over past misdeeds, must be subordinated to the urgent, immediate task. In this instance, the immediate task is the defeat of Nazi tyranny. If this task does not engage us, both our repentance and our hope become luxuries in which we indulge while other men save us from an intolerable fate, or while our inaction betrays into disaster a cause to which we owe allegiance.

In the Battle and Above It

[*Christianity and Society*, Vol. 7 (Autumn 1942), pp. 3–4.]

THERE are always Christians and other sensitive people who are convinced that it must be their business to be above the struggles and battles of history. They find the heat and the hatred of battle so terrible that refusal to participate in it seems to them the only possibility of maintaining any degree of decency and purity. There are on the other hand always other types, robust in temper and activist in ambition, who are "released" from self, and therefore "redeemed" by their complete devotion to a cause, such as only the pressure and crisis of battle can achieve. They attain a new degree of unselfishness in the patriotic preoccupations of war-time; and they may even compound some hatred of the enemy with this new found devotion to their country. This combination of love and hatred seems to satisfy both the lower and the higher instincts of their nature; and they have no need or desire to transcend the battle.

The true way of life is to be found in neither of these two strategies. There is no possibility of remaining aloof of all the battles of history without being a parasite upon those who fight the battles. Many Christians refuse to believe this because they imagine it possible to achieve and maintain justice in the world without the conflicts into which the tensions of justice periodically degenerate. But if we fully understand the precarious as well as precious character of even imperfect systems of justice, we will know that they must be defended, even if their defense involves us in tragic conflict. On the other hand, it is wrong for any Christian to be completely engulfed in battle.

To be in a battle means to defend a cause against its peril, to protect a nation against its enemies, to strive for truth against error, to defend justice against injustice. To be above the battle means that we understand how imperfect the cause is which we defend, that we contritely acknowledge the sins of our own nations, that we recognize the common humanity which binds us to even the most terrible foes, and that we know also of our common need of grace and forgiveness. To be above the battle must also mean some reverent and pitying comprehension of the vastness of the catastrophe which has engulfed us all, friend and foe, and some sense of pity for the victims of the struggle, whether ally or enemy. . . .

The Death of the President

[*Christianity and Crisis*, Vol. 5 (April 30, 1945), pp. 4–6.] After Franklin D. Roosevelt died on April 12, 1945, Niebuhr wrote this appreciation of his achievements and legacy.

THE American Presidency embodies two levels of political authority and prestige which a constitutional monarchy separates. The president is both king and prime minister. He symbolizes the perpetual authority of government as such but also embodies the immediate will of the nation as it becomes crystallized in party politics. The American Presidency has become the greatest single center of political power in the modern world. The death of a president, particularly of a great president, is therefore a great emotional shock to the nation. And since Mr. Roosevelt's authority and prestige transcended the boundaries of his own nation and he had become a symbol to the world of our nation's growing maturity and sense of responsibility toward the community of nations, his death has brought grief, and also some dismay and apprehension, to all the nations allied with us.

Our sense of grief is naturally mingled with gratitude for the providential emergence of this man in our national life at just such a time as this. There were those who tolerated his foreign policy because they believed in his domestic policy, while others tolerated or opposed his domestic policy while they supported his foreign policy. But in a word, his greatness, surely, was derived from the fact that he understood the essential issue in both domestic and foreign affairs. He was the first of our political leaders who sought to bring the immense powers of government to bear upon the economic health of the nation and thus to break with the *laissez-faire* tradition, which had a stronger hold upon us than on any other modern industrial nation. While many feared, or pretended to fear, the accretion of political power which resulted from this policy, no one can deal honestly with the issues involved in this controversy if he does not recognize that the increase of political power in a modern industrial community is prompted and justified by the desire of the community to bring the economic power of a technical society under communal control. The idea that economic power is self-regulating belongs to the childhood of an industrial era and is refuted by all of its maturer experience. Roosevelt was no systematic political thinker, but he saw the main issue clearly and acted upon his convictions with as much consistency as the confused state of American public opinion would allow. Even his lack of consistency and his infinite capacity for improvisation had their virtuous sides, for it is a question whether a more consistent or doctrinaire exponent of his policy could have achieved as much national unity around his central purpose as he achieved. While it is much too early to assess his place in American history adequately, one may hazard the guess that future historians will regard his administration as a new level of maturity in domestic policy. Here the nation became aware of the depth of the problems of justice in an industrial society and of the necessity of dealing with them politically.

In the same manner his foreign policy represented a new level of maturity in our relations to the world. Just as fabulous wealth had made it possible for us to evade the profounder economic issues a little longer than other nations, so, also, our continental security tempted us to evade the problems of an unorganized world. Roosevelt came to power a year before Hitler did and by a curious historical irony the two careers run chronologically parallel even to the point where one may hope that the one will not outlast the other by more than a few months. Roosevelt was President of a nation which had recoiled from its previous effort in international affairs and which was almost psychopathic in its determination to stay out of the conflict which Hitler's movement made inevitable; yet he understood the nature of the international crisis from the beginning. On this issue, as well as in domestic policy, his political ingenuity matched the clarity of his vision. The clarity of his vision was fully revealed in his famous "quarantine speech" in which he warned the world of the consequences of allowing aggression to go unchecked. His political sagacity dictated a course which would not outrun the sentiments of a divided nation too far. A lesser statesman might have abandoned himself to a sense of futility. Yet Roosevelt was able to secure the passage of the Lend-Lease Act from a divided nation, a policy which made it possible for us to prevent the collapse of the anti-Nazi cause, though a part of the nation was almost hysterically committed to the proposition that we had no responsibilities for the defeat of Nazism. Surely the passage of this act will go down in history as one of the greatest of his political achievements.

As the war finally drew to a triumphant conclusion, Roosevelt, seeking to avoid Wilson's mistakes, developed an international policy which, though it may err on the side of making too many concessions to the pride and power of the great nations, does at least guarantee that America will not again withdraw from its responsibilities in the world community. Nor can the concessions be regarded as merely unwarranted expediency. They are derived from a shrewd understanding of the limits of the will of a nation in creating international authority above its own sovereignty. In both the conduct of the war and in the peace negotiations Roosevelt has, in other words, expressed a higher form of political maturity than this nation has previously achieved. If the measures of international accord now being taken should prove inadequate, as indeed they may, the fault will lie not so much in the judgment of a man as in the historic situation. More adequate measures would have little chance of acceptance, either by our own nation or by the other great powers. . . .

The sense of grief in the nation has been mingled not only with gratitude for the greatness of the lost leader but with a good deal of apprehension about the future. Is the new President, or any untried man, adequate to fill so great an office in so trying a period of national history? No one can answer that question. One can only hope and pray that the greatness of the office may, as it has sometimes done in the past, develop unknown resources in the man.

The American Presidency has undoubtedly become too powerful. It may be worth observing that this is not exactly the fault of Mr. Roosevelt as his critics have averred. Given the American constitutional system, which does not provide for a "responsible government" in the parliamentary sense of that phrase, only a strong President can save the nation from disaster in times of crisis. A weak President in times of depression and war, such as we have traversed in the past decades, would not have increased the powers of his office. But our system does not function in such a way as to make it possible for Congress as such to master a crisis. Without a strong President disaster might well overwhelm us. We are not fully conscious of this fact because by great good fortune we have had great presidents in critical times. The fact that this cannot always be so may well fill us with apprehension about the future, but it will not qualify our gratitude for past mercies, among which belongs the leadership of Franklin Delano Roosevelt during this fateful decade of our history.

Soberness in Victory

[*Christianity and Crisis*, Vol. 5 (May 28, 1945), pp. 1–2.] Niebuhr here reflected on the defeat of Hitler's Germany early in May of 1945.

IT was most fortunate that America received the news of the victory in Europe more quietly than a quarter century ago. The hysteria of the former occasion was absent for various reasons. We had had several weeks to anticipate the victory, while the Nazi power gradually collapsed. There was a difference of a day between the actual and the official knowledge of the surrender; and furthermore the war was not over.

These were the immediate causes of our comparative soberness. But there were even profounder reasons for sobriety in victory. Perhaps they also affected the public mood; and perhaps they prompted the rather large attendance at religious services on V-E day. These reasons are all comprehended in the magnitude of the drama in which we are involved. Everything which is happening is really too big and too complex for our comprehension. The war which has ended in victory was the costliest and most global conflict of human history. It has left even the wealthiest victor nations shaken in the very structure of their economic life; and it has reduced Europe to a physical and economic as well as political chaos. The price of victory has been very high.

The defeated enemy has been more completely destroyed than any nation in history, at least since the day when the Romans destroyed Carthage. That was partly because the nation was ruled by a tyranny which was able to hold a beaten nation in battle until almost the last ounce of life blood was drawn from it. The same tyranny has also been able to destroy every crystallization of new political life during its long and terrible reign; so that Germany is a political vacuum as well as an economic desert. It is still a question whether our obliteration bombing, which has reduced the whole of western and central Germany to a rubble heap, was necessary for victory, though no less an authority than Von Runstedt has affirmed that precision bombing was indispensable to our victory. If it was necessary for victory we have another proof of the total character of total war.

The cost of this war has been so great for both victors and vanquished that many will undoubtedly arise to remind us of their predictions of its price and of their apprehensions about its consequences. We will have to remind them that some of their apprehensions were wrong. They had declared that we could not engage in this struggle without losing our democratic institutions. These have in fact survived the extraordinary exertions of the conflict very well. But it will be more important to call their attention to the fact that the war was an alternative to slavery. As the victorious armies liberated one concentration camp after another and unearthed the hideous cruelties which were practiced in them, they gave us some hint of what the dimensions of total slavery are like, from which we escaped by a total war.

However we measure the conflict, whether in terms of the evil we opposed, or the evils we had to commit in opposing it, or the destruction of the vanquished or the price of the victors, the dimensions of the drama in which we are involved are staggering. It is well that we should be shocked into sobriety by the magnitude of historical events and should be prompted to humility and piety by a contemplation of the tasks which still confront us. All of them are really beyond our best wisdom. . . .

Germans Who Are Not Nazis

[*The Messenger*, Vol. 11 (October 15, 1946), p. 6.] Niebuhr wrote this in the wake of a trip to Germany on an educational mission for the U.S. State Department in 1946.

ALL during the war there was speculation on the question of how many Germans were really Nazis. A small percentage of Americans insisted that all Germans were Nazis. Others felt that nazism was a conspiracy against the German people as much as a plot against the world. Still others believed that the truth lay somewhere between these extremes. And we lacked information to substantiate any conclusions.

The first statistics issued by the denazification section of our military government in Germany now give us some concrete evidence of the actual state of affairs. These statistics show that 5 per cent or about 3,500,000 Germans were explicit anti-Nazis. Fifty-one per cent had no connection with any Nazi organization. Of the remaining 44 per cent, only 17 per cent gave clear proof of being explicit Nazis.

The others were implicated in some Nazi organization, but frequently it was an organization such as a public welfare group, which the Nazis had taken over, and which some Germans felt bound to support for humane reasons, even though it was tainted at the top.

This is an interesting picture to which I may add some details after a discussion with many scores of Germans on the spot. One detail is that many Germans recognized the evil in Nazism earlier, and hated it more, than some of their present detractors. I have found no one who did not want every one of the Nuremberg criminals sentenced. I have in fact received a more vivid impression of the diabolical character of Nazism by talking to Germans, than I ever had, even though these Germans did not know some things about concentration camps which we knew.

Another detail is the religious vitality of both Protestant and Catholic churches in our part of Germany, in their opposition to Nazism. There were other parts of Germany where the opposition was primarily political. I do not wish to detract from the moral quality of this political opposition. But it is a fact that in the states of the American zone, that is, in Bavaria, Württemberg and Hesse, the religious life of the people was a strong resource against Nazism and preserved them from corruption. Sometimes this opposition rose to heroic proportions. But even when it was not heroic (and there are not many heroes in any nation) it was stubborn.

Even now, as one surveys the religious life of these people, one has the feeling that they compare more than favorably with their counterparts in any religion. They have been purified by suffering.

Germany as a powerful nation is dead, I think, for decades and possibly centuries. But we have not heard the last of her as a resource in the cultural and religious life of the western world.

The Organization of the Liberal Movement

[*Christianity and Society,* Vol. 12 (Spring 1947), pp. 8–10.] Niebuhr here described the purpose of Americans for Democratic Action after co-chairing its founding in January of 1947.

I HAVE been asked by my colleagues on the editorial board of *Christianity and Society* to give my estimate of the meaning of recent organizational developments in the liberal or progressive movement of America. These developments, most briefly stated, are the consolidation of two liberal organizations into the Progressive Citizens of America on the one hand, and the formation of Americans for Democratic Action on the other. I can, of course, give no completely disinterested account of these developments because I am . . . involved in the latter organization, and it grew out of plans and projects of the Union for Democratic Action, of which I have been chairman for the past six years. The new organization has the power and scope we always wanted our original group to have; but the time was not propitious until the present moment.

The difference between the two organizations is obvious. The Progressive Citizens has a large number of Communists and fellow travelers and beyond them the liberals who follow Henry Wallace's line in foreign policy. That line is very critical of our present foreign policy on the ground that it would be in the interest of peace to yield to the Russians on quite a few points. . . . There is room for criticism here of our foreign policy which I hope liberals will press. On the whole, however, Americans for Democratic Action agrees with the administration policy of "patience and firmness" toward Russia, believing that the Wallace type of liberalism inclines to make the same mistakes about Russia which the right made in regard to Germany. That mistake is to suppose that a dictatorship can be beguiled by concessions when actually it hopes to overcome its strategic weakness by scaring the democracies into concessions.

We believe, of course, that mere firmness on strategic issues does not suffice and that a liberal movement must press the government to adopt economic policies which will assure the economic health of Germany and Western Europe. If we fail in this, Russia will ultimately conquer Europe ideologically. We do not believe that the unification of Europe under Russian power would make for peace. If Russia came within proximate sight of that goal, there would be war. It is therefore in the interest of peace that we would have the American progressive movement resist Russian expansion on the Continent.

On the other hand, we believe that an American progressive movement must resist the American reactionaries who would be glad to have a practical state of war between Russia and the West, and who might not even be averse to a preventive war whenever it became apparent that Russia had the bomb. We do not believe that war between the West and Russia is either imminent or inevitable. . . .

The ADA promises to become an important common effort not only between middle class liberals and labor, but between the AFL and the CIO. . . . The new organization probably represents the great bulk of American liberal opinion. If it succeeds in giving that opinion organizational cohesion, it will isolate the Communist-influenced liberalism, allowing it only such strength as it may honestly claim. In the past the latter has always pretended to speak for the whole of labor and liberal opinion. This led to a dangerous confusion in foreign policy and to an unnecessary discrediting of liberal opinion in the eyes of the nation. Whenever liberals became apprehensive about this situation they were told that they must not join the reactionary "red baiters."

To maintain a middle ground between the reaction of the right and the left requires that an independent policy be developed without regard to such apprehensions. The situation in the whole Western world would be improved if the fear of Communism did not drive some people into the arms of reaction, and the fear of reaction did not drive others into the arms of Communism. Both fears must be overcome by the development of a healthy democratic program, embracing both foreign and domestic policy and both economic and political problems.

American Power and European Health

[*Christianity and Crisis*, Vol. 7 (June 9, 1947), pp. 1–2.] Niebuhr wrote this piece days before Secretary of State George Marshall's Harvard address proposing the plan for European economic recovery that bears his name.

AMERICAN power is so dominant in the Western world that every problem of European destiny must wait for its solution upon some American decision. We may make a right decision on one level of policy and still wreck the European future because we fail to carry through with other necessary decisions. So far we have made one right decision; but it is not yet certain whether we will make the others.

The one right decision we have made is our evident intention to stay in Europe and prevent the Russian power from inundating the European continent. We may or may not agree with the specific policy taken in Greece and Turkey; but Europe was, on the whole, right in appreciating primarily the symbolic significance of that action. It was a symbol of our determination to remain in Europe, though there might well have been a more adequate token of this determination than what was actually done in Greece and Turkey.

It is significant however that even now Europe is still apprehensive about our future policy. It is afraid that an economic depression at home might tempt us to withdraw from our commitments. That is why Barbara Ward, the foreign editor of *The Economist*, after a recent tour of America, rightly came to the conclusion that the future of Europe will be largely determined by the health of the American economy. Here an element in human history above or below the level of conscious decision is revealed. No matter what we want to do or what we say we will do, we will not do it if we lose our power. An American depression will be, not merely a social catastrophe for us, but a calamity for the world. It may be worth noting that the Russians are speculating daily on the possibility and the imminence of this depression. Their stubbornness on many issues is partly prompted by the hope that, if they are patient enough, we will in time pull out of Europe so that they can move in.

But even if our will and our power to remain in Europe should remain unyielding, we must make another decision on a higher level of policy. We must, as Under Secretary Acheson recently insisted, offer Europe, including Great Britain, much more economic support than hitherto contemplated. Mr. Acheson suggested a peacetime lease-lend arrangement of five billion dollars annually. Such a decision will require a very high measure of political imagination. Our treatment of Britain in the British loan negotiations does not encourage too much confidence in our ability to rise to such a level of political wisdom. The whole of western Europe is sinking in an economic morass. If there is no economic convalescence in Europe there can be no restored political health. The economic aid which is required could not be a matter of pure generosity. Nations as nations are incapable of such generosity. We could rise to such a policy only if we were wise enough to understand that generous, interest-free loans would not merely save the economy of western Europe but would also insure our own economic health. We have only begun to realize the difficulties of relating the economy of a very wealthy nation to that of a very impoverished world.

But even such economic farsightedness will not avail if we do not implement our policy by one further step. We must restore the economic health of Europe without trying to dictate the political organization of European nations. Europe seeks desperately to avoid totalitarianism; but both Britain and the continent are much too impoverished to regard our uncritical identification of free enterprise with democracy as anything but an irrelevance at best and as a peril at worst. It is not easy for a nation to exercise its power without using it to enforce its prejudices. Our excessively libertarian interpretations of democracy are a prejudice as far as Europe is concerned. If we insist upon them Europe may be wrecked even though we meet all other tests.

One final and necessary element in our policy is not so much a matter of conscious decision as of the temper and mood in which our conscious decisions are made. We cannot afford the hysteria to which those are tempted who understand the perils of our day, any more than we can afford the complacency of those who are blind to our perils. Hysterical talk about the inevitability of a third world war and the necessity of preparing for it is just as irresponsible as the policy of yielding to tyranny in order to avoid war. We are fated to live for a long while in a world in which no stable peace can be guaranteed; but it does not follow that a war is either inevitable or desirable. We can do our duty in this kind of world only if we are as sober as we are firm. It is worth observing that the whole of modern culture, with its promise of quick and sure results for the right action has not prepared us for this kind of moral experience. This nation must draw upon the resources of the Christian faith if we would do our duty each day without too many fearful apprehensions and too many unjustified hopes about tomorrow. "Sufficient unto the day are the evils thereof." That can only be said from the standpoint of a faith which understands the eternal depth in every moment of time, and the intrinsic meaning of every duty undertaken under God.

The Sin of Racial Prejudice

[*The Messenger,* Vol. 13 (February 3, 1948), p. 6.] Niebuhr addressed the problem of racial prejudice now and again, beginning in 1927 after he chaired a mayor's committee on race relations in Detroit and continuing through the decades as that social sin took various forms in America and elsewhere.

I HAVE, as a teacher of youth, noticed that in recent years the morally and socially sensitive students have become more and more conscious of the evils of racial bigotry. A decade ago they were preoccupied with problems of economic injustice. There is, it seems to me, a real justification for this shift in interest.

The economic problems which were our concern a decade ago have, of course, not been solved but only obscured by wartime and postwar prosperity. It is apparent that we will face the full force of the economic problem in the not too distant future. But past decades were quite wrong in ascribing every form of social evil to economics.

It was assumed, for instance, that racial friction was merely the by-product of economic unrest, and would disappear if the economic problem were solved. Gunnar Myrdal, in his great study of American racial issues entitled *An American Dilemma*, has made the most cogent refutation of this erroneous thesis. Furthermore, our present experience is refuting it. For we are living in a period of comparative economic complacency but of rising racial friction.

Economic injustice in a technical society arises from the tendencies of such a society toward great disproportions of economic power. But the sins of pride are probably more stubborn in human affairs than the sins of power. Injustices arising from disproportion of power can be cured by establishing a greater equilibrium of power. But the evils which are derived from human pride are more spiritual and stubborn.

The sense of racial superiority means that a particular kind of man, white or black, Jew or Gentile, Occidental or Oriental, forgets the conditioned character of his life and culture and pretends that his color, creed or culture represents some kind of final and absolute criterion of the good. He proceeds thereupon to judge other people severely who do not conform to his particular standard.

This is a pathetic and dangerous fallacy; but it is one in which almost all men are involved in varying degrees. It cannot be cured merely by a shift in a given social equilibrium. It can be mitigated by educational programs, designed to reveal the relative character of all human cultures, and the excellencies in forms of life other than our own.

But the mitigation of racial and cultural pride is finally a religious problem in the sense that each man, and each race and culture, must become religiously aware of the sin of self-worship, which is the final form of human evil and of which racial self-worship is the most vivid example.

We are not God. We are only creatures. All creatures are conditioned by climate and geography and by every special circumstance. Religious humility, as well as rational enlightenment, must contribute to the elimination of this terrible evil of racial pride.

Halfway to What?

[*The Nation*, Vol. 170 (January 14, 1950), pp. 26–28.]

THE embattled American plutocracy, finding political power slipping from its hands and seeing little in the whole world to give it comfort, has invented a nice little theory to scare its enemies and quiet its own apprehensions. This is that the policies of the New Deal or the Fair Deal are a halfway house to socialism, even as socialism is a halfway house to communism and totalitarianism. Any nation, therefore, which uses its sovereign power to extend the general welfare is starting down the slippery slope which ends in the abyss of totalitarianism. At a recent convention of the National Association of Manufacturers almost every speaker reiterated this idea until it became a kind of liturgy. . . . John T. Flynn has recently invented a variant of the theory. British socialism, he declares, is a halfway house to *either* fascism or communism. It has no other choice.

The idea is too implausible to have much political effect. The danger is that it may so blind American business men to real trends that they will understand the world they live in as little as the bosses of the Kremlin, who wear another set of blinders. Our business men, to be sure, are not so powerful as the Communist oligarchs, but they are not impotent, and they might in their blindness become dangerous. We ought to do our best, therefore, to enlighten them.

In this task the first point to emphasize is that no nation in modern history has ever lost its liberties by inadvertence. No people has ever used a free election to annul the power of its suffrage. Totalitarian systems are forced upon nations in times of social convulsion, when minorities of either the right or the left have found it possible to seize control of the government. Aware that a free election would never validate their authority, these minorities have destroyed democracy, either with the complete cynicism of the Nazis or the combined cynicism and illusion of the Communists.

It must be noted, in the second place, that the Socialist and quasi-Socialist regimes which seek to control economic life through the democratic process have impaired the liberties of their peoples so little that two such governments, in Australia and in New Zealand, have just been defeated in an election. . . .

This does not mean that every detail of democratic socialism is defensible or that the successive steps toward the political control of economic processes in America are always justified. But whatever the differences between the United States and the Socialist and quasi-Socialist nations of the Continent, we have in common the will to use political power to mitigate the injustices which arise from the increased centralization of economic power inherent in a technical society. Thus political movements driven solely by the resentments of the defrauded and intent upon a revolutionary overthrow of society are not required. Society moves from point to point toward a more tolerable justice.

The nostalgia of the American business community for the "never-never land" of pure laissez faire is doubly ironic. In the first place, the business community sought, as long as it could, to bend political power to its ends, violating every principle of free enterprise. The tariff policy of the Republican Party is certainly not in harmony with the principles of laissez faire; nor were such devices as the Reconstruction Finance Corporation, which, originally conceived in the Hoover era, was designed to bail out some of the weakest units of American business. Protests rose against the use of political power in economic life when the masses began to use it to broaden their economic opportunities, to check the centralization of economic power, and to assure basic economic security. The American business community tried desperately to prove the truth of the Marxist theory that political power is always the slave of the dominant economic power. The theory was refuted through the discovery by the common people that their political power could be used to redress economic imbalances.

Business nostalgia is also ironic because the movement away from the pure theory and the impure practice of free enterprise actually saved modern democratic nations from the social convulsions with their totalitarian outcome which occurred in less democratic nations. This movement invalidated not only the Marxist dogma of the inevitable subservience of political to economic power but the ancillary doctrine that an imperiled privileged class would inevitably embark on fascist adventures to destroy the democracy which endowed the people with dangerous political power. No fascist adventures were resorted to in Britain, or in Norway or Sweden, or in Australia or New Zealand. It is possible, in short, for nations to have so strong a sense of community beyond and above the class conflict that a minority will yield its privileges without seeking to destroy the majority's political power. The minority submits in healthy democratic nations partly because it has a sense of justice beyond its class interests and partly because the authority of government is great enough to make a rebellion of either the right or the left too precarious.

In America no full-fledged Marxist movement has ever developed. If the lack of one retarded the political development of the working classes here, it also freed American labor from many Marxist illusions which European labor parties carry as so much excess baggage. The highly pragmatic and not very consistent policies of the New Deal first showed the American people how to use political power for correcting economic abuses. But the election of Truman was more instructive than anything which happened in the Roosevelt era. For here a candidate, seemingly doomed to defeat, saved himself by embracing the cause of the common man more unambiguously than Roosevelt ever did.

The movement toward basic economic security for the common man in America is too pragmatic to satisfy British Socialists, even as the British have always been too lax in their dogmas to satisfy their more orthodox colleagues on the Continent. But the British and Scandinavian Socialists have carried the national communities with them, while the orthodox Continental parties have never succeeded in gaining any great mass of adherents outside the industrial workers. The democratic middle ground on the Continent must therefore be held by an uneasy alliance between working-class parties encumbered with Marxist dogma and middle-class parties controlled by ecclesiastical interests. No one can doubt the sincerity of the Socialist devotion to freedom and opposition to communism. But the Socialists regard Stalinism as a corruption of the original Marxist dream. They do not fully recognize that this corruption is the natural fruit of certain Marxist illusions. The most grievous of these illusions is the expectation that the proletarian state will wither away, for this inclines men toward an uncritical acceptance of an allegedly temporary dictatorship.

Pragmatism as such has no particular virtue. There must be a proper framework of values in which pragmatic decisions are reached. The democratic movement, whether Socialist or non-Socialist, finds this framework in devotion to justice and freedom and in a recognition that while every form of power, whether political or economic, must be made to serve the cause of justice, the very exercise of power imperils justice.

Many modern democracies which have placed checks upon economic power have sacrificed no essential freedom, not even the freedom of the nation to reverse the tendency toward greater control of economic life. It does not follow, however, that the indeterminate extension of political control over life is necessarily wise. On the contrary, it may be unwise, not because a tyrannical state is thus inadvertently created, as the conservatives maintain, but because bureaucratic decisions can never anticipate all the economic contingencies which a free market holds in some kind of harmony. A nation might preserve all its essential political liberties and yet become economically sterile. Society will always face the problem of "achieving the harmony of the whole without destroying the vitality of the parts." We don't know exactly how to achieve this end and must therefore proceed circumspectly. We only know that a completely free market lacks the self-regulating power once ascribed to it, and that too inclusive planning destroys the flexibility which a healthy economy requires.

The extension of political control over economic life may also be unwise if it rests upon the assumption that man's social needs, whether for basic security, housing, education, or health, are determinate. All human needs are indeterminate. As a consequence inordinate demands are bound to be made upon any political scheme which offers "free" services. A modern democracy must provide health insurance for all of its citizens; that is one way in which the sovereign power of a government ought to be used. It may well be, however, that the British health scheme contains too many Marxist assumptions about the determinate character of human needs. The health schemes of our most progressive unions are more circumspect, and we may hope that state-supported schemes will be equally so.

The highly pragmatic type of progressive democracy developing in America, which is condemned by the reactionaries as a halfway house to communism and criticized even by British Socialists as lacking in dogmatic rigor, may prove better able to preserve democratic justice in a technical society than any of the alternatives of right or left. This can be our answer to Europeans who criticize the ambiguities of our political life. To our own reactionary critics we must emphasize the common elements in the democratic life of Europe and America. The democratic movement in America is not slipping into totalitarianism. It is the only effective safeguard against totalitarianism.

The Hydrogen Bomb

[*Christianity and Society*, Vol. 15 (Spring 1950), pp. 5–7.] After news in 1949 that Soviet Russia had the atomic bomb, Niebuhr supported the American government's decision to develop the more deadly hydrogen bomb as a deterrent, on the assumption that Russia would develop it also.

EACH age of mankind brings forth new perils and new possibilities. Yet they are always related to what we have known before. The age of atomic bombs, suddenly developing into a thousand times more lethal hydrogen bombs, is very different from the age of scythe and plowshare. It confronts us with the possibility of mutual mass annihilation. Yet we are no different from our fathers. Our present situation is a heightened and more vivid explication of the human situation.

One basic similarity between ourselves and our fathers is that our power over the course of human history is limited. We had imagined that the very technics that finally produced atomic destruction would make us the masters of history. But they merely produce an increased amount of power over nature that has a dubious role in the affairs of men. When we confront the problem of bringing the destructive possibilities of this power under moral control, the whole ambiguity of the human situation is more fully revealed.

Consider the facts. We had the knowledge to produce the more lethal bomb four years ago, but wisely did not exploit it. Then, when the news came that the Russians had the A-bomb, we were certain that they would be, as we were, on the way to achieving the more deadly H-bomb. There seemed, therefore, nothing to do but give orders to develop it. The fact that this was done without public debate represents a real threat to the democratic substance of our life. This merely accentuates the danger in which we have been ever since secret weapons have been developed. It is, at any rate, fairly certain that, had the President submitted the matter to Congress, the decision would have been identical with the one he made. Thus we have come into the tragic position of developing a form of destruction which, if used by our enemies against us, would mean our physical annihilation; and if used by us against our enemies, would mean our moral annihilation. What shall we do?

The pacifists have a simple answer. Let us simply renounce the use of such a weapon, together with our enemies if possible, but alone if necessary. This answer assumes that it is possible to summon the human will to defy historical development with a resounding no. But where is this "human will" which could rise to such omnipotence? Unfortunately we do not have moral access to the Russian will. We have to limit ourselves to the will of America and of the Western world. Could we possibly, as a nation, risk annihilation or subjugation for the sake of saying no to this new development of destruction? Could we risk letting the Russians have the bomb while we are without it? The answer is that no responsible statesman will risk putting his nation in that position of defenselessness. Individuals may, but nations do not, thus risk their very existence. Would a gesture of defenselessness possibly soften the Russian heart? That is the other possibility implied in the pacifist solution. The answer is that we have no such assurance. Granted the Russian hope and belief that it has the possibility of bringing its peculiar redemption to the whole world, it is not likely to be impressed by any "moral" gesture from what it believes to be a decadent world. In other words, our will is neither powerful enough nor good enough to accomplish the miracle expected of us in the pacifist solution. . . .

Perhaps the most feasible possibility is that proposed by a group of eleven scientists who have suggested that we produce the H-bomb but make a solemn covenant never to use it first. This proposal has several merits. It would serve to allay some of the apprehensions that the world feels about our possible use of the bomb. It would also restrain those elements in our defense department who are placing undue reliance on the bomb and who may, if we are not careful, so develop our defenses that we could not win a war without using the bomb. It would also tend to counteract all those tendencies in our national life which make for the subordination of moral and political strategy to military strategy. We must not forget that, though we must be prepared to defend ourselves in case of war, it is more important to overcome communism by moral, economic, and political measures. In that case we would not have to fight the war for which the strategists are preparing our defenses. For this reason the proposals of Senator McMahon, looking toward a tremendous expansion of our aid to the Western world, are of great significance.

The refusal to use the bomb first is not of itself a sufficient strategy. But such a refusal would tend to encourage all the more positive strategies for preserving both peace and civilization. Yet the refusal to use the bomb first does have a further significance. We would be saying by such a policy that even a nation can reach the point where it can purchase its life too dearly. If we had to use this kind of destruction in order to save our lives, would we find life worth living? Even nations can reach a point where the words of our Lord, "Fear not them which are able to kill the body but rather fear them that are able to destroy both soul and body in hell," become relevant.

The point of moral transcendence over historical destiny is not as high as moral perfectionists imagine. But there is such a point, though the cynics and realists do not recognize it. We must discern that point clearly. A nation does not have the power to say that it would rather be annihilated than to produce a certain weapon. For, as the scientists have asserted, the production of that weapon may serve to guarantee that it will never be used. But to use such a weapon first represents a quite different moral hazard. It ought not to be impossible for nations to meet that hazard successfully.

Television's Peril to Culture

[*The American Scholar,* Vol. 19 (Spring 1950), pp. 137–40.] Television had just begun to appear on the American scene when Niebuhr wrote this piece on its deleterious effects.

THE first great achievement of the art of communication was the invention of writing. Further developments through the ages have produced the invention of printing and of the wireless, and now, most recently, television. Since the invention of writing was one of the most important of those propulsive forces which transmuted barbarism into civilization, we have assumed, rather uncritically, that each new technical advance in communication must have as creative a relation to the cultural development of mankind as the first. But the very ambiguous effect of television upon our contemporary culture may force us to revise our estimates.

Television may not be as dangerous to culture as the atomic bomb is to our civilization. (The atomic bomb is related to the plow in the history of the conquest of nature as television is related to writing in the history of communications.) But this last word in the art of communication seems suddenly to illumine a disturbing aspect of this history which we had not sufficiently noted. Each new development in the art of communication seems to have broadened the base of culture on the one hand and to have vulgarized the arts on the other.

The technical triumphs of moving pictures cannot obscure the difference between the maturity of the art of the drama and the infantilism of Hollywood art. There is, however, an important difference between the vulgarization of art in moving pictures and the vulgarizations of television. Sentimentality and vulgarity in the movies are not caused by any limitations in the medium itself. They stem rather from the effort of a mass medium to hold a mass audience by gauging its appeal to the lowest common denominator of aesthetic receptivity.

The case of television is more complicated and a little more hopeless than that of the movies; for some of the limitations spring from the medium itself. The comedy currently popular on television is almost completely bereft of any genuine wit or humor. This may be partly a result of the fact that a television chain, fighting desperately to make both ends meet, strives for a maximum audience for each program. Again, it may be that only the most obvious kind of slapstick is sufficiently vivid visually. At any rate, the descent from Fred Allen to Milton Berle is, for the moment at least, the measure of the difference between radio and television humor. It must be noted also that technical limitations make the presentation of genuine dramatic art on television difficult. Sports are more popular on television than drama; and the prize fight seems to be the most acceptable sport, because it conforms best to the limitations of the camera's eye.

Many of the technical difficulties will, no doubt, be overcome in time. We are rightly reminded that television is in its infancy. Its present estate may have the same relation to a subsequent state of perfection as the nickelodeon has to the present cinema. But even this comparison is not too reassuring. It suggests that in each new technical development of mass communications, the new medium is gradually mastered; but the highest state of perfection is still below the artistic level of a previous period in which there was less preoccupation with the mass "outlets" of the medium.

Television affords an even more serious threat to culture in terms of the communication of ideas than it does in the projection of artistic images. The discussion of public issues and the dissemination of ideas on the radio represent an almost clear gain, since radio has augmented communication through the written word without vulgarization. We must admit, of course, that the radio has given modern tyrannies a new weapon by piping Dr. Goebbels' or Stalin's propaganda into every home. But the content and form of discussion on television is on an obviously lower level of maturity. Visual aids, graphs and maps are introduced into the discussion even when they are only slightly relevant. What is worse, discussion topics seem to be chosen not because they are important but because they lend themselves to visual elaboration. There is, furthermore, considerable preoccupation with the posture of speakers, their facial expressions and all manner of irrelevant considerations. A television discussion is a studied effort to present a scene of unstudied conversation in which the visual effects are regarded as much more important than the content of the discussion. If the speakers are also constantly warned against the use of words which might not be understood by a tenth grade child, this proves that some of the difficulties arise not from the limitations of the medium but from preoccupation with the mass audience. Television will have to learn that, even in the most democratic culture, it is simply not possible to address everybody on every subject.

All these apprehensions may seem to be dictated by a too aristocratic concept of culture, which lacks a proper appreciation of the immense benefits which mass communications confer upon "the masses" by making every treasure of culture more widely available. There is some merit in such a democratic criticism. But one must also consider the degree to which the "common" men of every age have an unspoiled art and a simple culture, upon which the artificialities and sentimentalities of the mass media may have a deleterious effect. Pretending to serve hypothetical mass tastes, they actually contaminate them. Furthermore, the mass media of the present day tend to destroy the inner core of a cultural discipline by their too frantic efforts at popularization. Even a democratic culture cannot afford an equalitarianism which threatens the sources of discipline of the mind and heart by trying to bring them *down* to the lowest common denominator.

It is possible that some of the cultural defects of the mass media, revealed in the movies and radio and accentuated in television, can be cured if there is a less immediate relation between commercial and cultural interests. Americans are rather too uncritically proud of the advantages of the "free enterprise system," including the advantages of competition in radio and television programs. There are indeed some advantages if comparison is made with the programs of the

British Broadcasting Corporation, for instance. But on the other hand there is nothing in American radio so consistently mature as the "Third Program" of the BBC, which is frankly designed for the more thoughtful tenth of the population. There is increasing evidence that a public service corporation of the type of the BBC will have a similar advantage in television, in furnishing adult entertainment for adults and mature discussions for mature minds.

Insofar as the inanities of television are derived from limitations in the medium itself, we may well expect these to be overcome as the medium is technically perfected. Insofar as they spring from a preoccupation with the mass audience and an unwillingness to cater for higher cultural needs, they must be corrected by destroying the too intimate relation between the advertiser and the medium. The assumed "automatic" controls of the competitive process are inoperative because they result in purely quantitative, rather than qualitative criteria of excellence. Television is on the same cultural level as "throwaway" newspapers in which the news and cultural content of the journal is a mere adjunct to the commercial ends of the advertisers. Since we do have excellent journals which have managed to achieve standards, which are only occasionally and incidentally corrupted by commercial pressure, we may reasonably hope for a similar development in radio and television. It may even be possible to achieve this end without resorting to the expedient of a public service monopoly. It is, however, a much more difficult end to achieve in radio and television, because no newspaper is forced to reach the "total market" in the same way as the newer mass media. . . .

The Poverty of Asia and Communism

[*Christianity and Society,* Vol. 16 (Winter 1950–51), pp. 6–8.]

IT is one of the ironies of history that the Communist creed, intended for the industrial workers of the Western world, should find the greatest acceptance among the agrarian poor. The Russian revolution was possible because a small group of Communists were able to manipulate the discontent of the landless peasants of Russia. They harnessed peasant support by promising land to the landless. Only later, after the instruments of political power were in Communist hands, did they reveal to the peasants that land would be taken away from them again and they would become "workers" in the vast "grain factories" of collective farms.

The political struggle against Communism in Asia is steadily deteriorating because the various creeds of democracy seem to have less appeal to the landless poor of Asia than does communism. Meanwhile the final fruits of communism, its tyranny and coercion, are hid from Asian eyes, except as China gradually learns what communism means in practice.

The Communist appeal to the landless poor seems particularly plausible precisely because it contains only a modicum of truth. The poverty of low grade agrarian economies is primarily due to low productivity. The most exacting system of justice would not give plenty to the people of Asia. There would not be enough bread or rice to go around even if it were distributed with perfect equity. In such a situation the injustices of landlordism and usurious interest rates are of course the more galling. But these injustices are not, in the exact sense of the word, due to "capitalistic exploitation." They represent pre-capitalistic injustice. Meanwhile Asia did come under capitalistic pressure. Its lack of technical power brought it into political subjection to Western powers. This political subjection inevitably created national and ethnic resentments. But it may be questioned whether "capitalistic exploitation" added anything to the poverty of Asia. Certainly orthodox Marxism has tended to over-emphasize both the economic motives and consequences of imperialism. As regards motives, an "imperialist" of the type of Churchill was certainly more interested in the prestige of empire than in the cash nexus. It would be difficult to prove that the higher technical proficiency which Holland introduced into Indonesia, and Britain into India, and America into the Philippines increased the poverty of these colonial nations, though it must certainly be admitted that the technical tutors appropriated more of the increased productivity for themselves than a decent rule of justice would allow.

Developing technics did not raise living standards as much as they might have because there was "exploitation." Nevertheless the capitalistic exploitation did not approach the injustice of the landlordism and interest slavery which is the indigenous injustice of agrarian economies from the time of Babylon and Egypt to the modern day. But even the elimination of the traditional injustice of agrarian societies would not bring physical well-being to Asia. Its power of production is too low. Furthermore its birth rate is too high.

The development of a technical society is a long process, particularly if the society is so poor that it has difficulty in finding money for initial investment in machinery. What therefore is more plausible and satisfying than a creed which attributes all this poverty to exploitation? If, furthermore, it is attributed to "foreign" exploitation one may live in the illusion that "independence" will bring prosperity. The illusion must of course be finally dispelled by the facts. Some of the recently emancipated nations of Asia are now in the process of this disillusionment.

These nations are free of capitalistic exploitation. But their political system has not always proved strong enough to overcome the traditional exploitation. Thus MacArthur initiated a more thoroughgoing land reform program in Japan than the "democratic" government of South Korea was able or willing to enforce. In this situation of disillusion and despair communism preaches hatred of the "capitalistic imperialists" and tries to prove that our billions of Marshall plan and other aid are a part of this system of exploitation. Only a modicum of facts fits the theory. But the theory fits the prejudices of Asia, particularly its rightful resentments against the pride and arrogance of the white civilization. Clearly the spiritual concomitants of "imperialism," the pride and prejudice of the "masters" have been more evil than the economic consequences. These predispose the poor Asians to accept an interpretation of the causes of their economic condition which is 90 per cent untrue. . . .

Will We Resist Injustice?

[*Christianity and Crisis,* Vol. 13 (April 13, 1953), pp. 41–42.] During the early 1950s Niebuhr, as in this piece, deplored Senator Joseph McCarthy's demagogic exploitation of public fears of Communism.

THOUGHTFUL observers will gratefully record that the administration, after trying to yield to McCarthy's pressure, has finally decided to resist him. Critics will affirm that he left no other recourse; for nothing short of allowing him a veto over all of its appointments would satisfy him. He proved that it makes no difference to him whether Dulles or Acheson is Secretary of State. He has shown that he knows no loyalty to the party and that his aberrations are not due to an excess of patriotic zeal so much as to his discovery that the fears of the nation represent a resource which he can exploit for political and personal advantage. . . .

A view of his investigation on television enables one to discern the peculiar flavor of his demagogic tricks as no newspaper account can transmit it. His technique consists in piling innuendo upon innuendo, and in raking the victim's past despite clear evidence that the past represents some youthful heresy long since atoned for by honorable and rigorous devotion to our democratic principles. Truth and justice are, in short, not in him. It is sad to note that there are not in the resources of this youthful nation the same instinctive reactions to an unjust act, especially to an unjust act by an organ of government, which characterizes the healthier European democracies. If there were, McCarthy could not have prospered so long among us and would not face so hopeful a prospect in the art of demagogy. . . .

The quality of justice in our Congressional investigations has long since been a special problem in our national life. Long before McCarthy came on the scene, these investigations tended to affront the conscience of the nation and to offend our friends in the free world because they lacked the safeguards against unjust accusations which are the fruits of a long history of democratic jurisprudence. Many of us will remember the odious record of the so-called Dies Committee. The age of McCarthy has given the dangers inherent in these investigations a wider scope while McCarthy's tactics have proved anew how necessary such safeguards are. Since Congressional investigations quite obviously have validity and function in our democracy, a way must be found to make them genuine instruments of justice before they corrupt the conscience of our people and threaten their liberties.

The Moral and Spiritual Content of the Atlantic Community

[*Five Years of the North Atlantic Alliance* (New York: American Council on NATO, 1954), pp. 25–30.] Niebuhr here reflected on the commonalities of tradition and the historic role of member nations in the North Atlantic Treaty Organization (NATO), established in 1949 to counter threatened expansion of Soviet power in Europe.

HISTORIC communities are founded on the one hand by the pressures and exigencies of history; and on the other hand by common culture and common aspirations. If these two factors are necessary for the stability of a community, the Atlantic community is assured stability; for it possesses both factors. The immediate pressure of history was the necessity of a common defense against tyranny. That peril caused the drawing together of the nations. The common danger prompted not only the common defense measures of NATO but also mutual economic measures, which would make the necessary rearmament measures economically viable. But even the direct common peril will not fashion a community if there is not some common stuff in its culture.

What makes the Atlantic community so exciting, and its integration so thrilling, is that this "common stuff" is not so much a unified culture, as a way of making diversity tolerable under conditions of freedom. The Atlantic community is sometimes described as a bastion of "Christian" civilization. But it contains many elements which are not strictly speaking Christian. It embraces the highly industrialized nations of Western Europe and the North American offshoots of Western European culture. It is difficult to say whether the industrialization and technical efficiency of these nations is the cause, or the consequence, of the "openness" of the society. At any rate, the culture has its base in a highly efficient technical civilization, the product of modern science. In terms of "culture" (if we may distinguish culture from civilization as we distinguish spirit from body), the Atlantic community is composed of nations who have discovered the way to community despite diversity. The diversity is created by the power of various versions of the Christian faith, by the Jewish faith and by various forms of secularism, some quasi-Christian and some anti-Christian. It must be admitted that community is not possible if the divergencies in culture and religion are too great. The failure of India to achieve a united nation in its freedom from Britain is a recent proof of the hazards of religious diversity to community. Fortunately the underlying unities below the diversities in the Atlantic community are very great. The religions are all derived from Biblical faith. The secularism does not seriously challenge the main ethical affirmations of the faith. On the other hand, its sciences implement the affirmative attitude toward human life and history which characterize that faith.

The underlying unity can not, of course, obviate the problems created by the diversities. The nations have a long history of gradually achieved toleration. This toleration was partly the consequence of a genuine passion for liberty, but also the product of necessity, once the cultural uniformity of the medieval period was broken and religious and cultural diversity was established. As our founding fathers, many of the European nations were prompted to adopt the hazardous step of allowing diversity because they saw the futility of getting back to the old uniformity by sheer coercion. Thus the nations of the Atlantic community all learned by sheer necessity that community under conditions of diversity was possible.

They also learned that it was desirable. An advantage of a free society, which no one quite anticipated, was that each group could make some contributions from its standpoint which no other group could quite make; and the pretensions of each group were challenged by the criticisms of other groups. This perpetual challenge to the pretensions of each group is one of the most wholesome effects of a free society. The advantages of democratic forms could hardly have been established, for instance, if the religious groups had not contributed the two prerequisites of a free society: the insistence that the individual has a dignity which makes it impossible for any community to use him as a mere instrument of its common purposes, and that he has a higher authority to inform his conscience than the necessities of the community; and if the whole realm of secular learning had not addressed the mind of man to the problems of human togetherness and had not traced the causes and consequences of human action to the end of excluding tyranny and monopoly of power as viable forms of community.

It is significant that these covenanted free communities have allowed the free play of political interests as well as religious convictions. A higher justice has evolved from this free play than more traditional societies have ever achieved. Most significant, perhaps, is that the very dogma, which in its pure form, has resulted in the tyranny against which we must now contend, was transmuted under the conditions of a free society into one of the instruments and forces of justice, so that the democratic socialism of European nations has been incorporated into the creative force of a free society, while it has become an instrument of tyranny in the social situation provided by decaying feudal agrarian orders.

It may seem arbitrary to organize a "North Atlantic Treaty Organization," which cuts across Europe on the one hand, and takes in two powerful nations on the other side of the Atlantic. But in this respect, too, the spiritual facts correspond to the strategic necessities. For the two North American nations are spiritual offshoots of the European community. Their power and strategic resource is therefore rightly dedicated to the necessities of a common defense. The East European nations, on the other hand, have been separated from this spiritual community on the one hand simply by the power of Russian arms in, or adjacent to, them. But on the other hand they lacked, with one exception, the political and cultural prerequisites for the open society, which characterizes the nations of NATO. History never presents us with neat coincidences of various forces. There is therefore no complete coincidence between the strategic necessities and the spirit which informs these communities. Some nations, sharing our general tradition have, for reasons of their own, refused to join this particular community of common defense. On the other hand, other nations are strategically necessary to it, even if they only partly share the political and moral heritage. But given the illogicalities of history, there is nevertheless a remarkable overlapping of political heritage and strategic common purpose in the North Atlantic Treaty Organization.

The conviction grows that the opportunity to practice in their international relations the principles which have slowly evolved in the domestic life of the several nations, constitutes this common adventure into more than a military enterprise and makes it into a genuine venture in community under conditions of freedom on the international level.

We face problems of global proportions, for the solution of which we require the resources of all nations. Nevertheless, it is significant that what had been generally defined as "Western civilization"—and which is characterized by technical efficiency and a consequent economic power, by respect for the individual, by the self-limitation of governments in dealing with the individual, and by the achievement of justice through an equilibrium of social and political forces—that it is this civilization which informs the life of the NATO nations, and that through them it is dedicated both to the preservation of its standards in their homelands and to an extension of those standards upon the higher level of international community.

The double purpose of the NATO community is important. Its purpose is, on the one hand, to protect the cherished values of the civilization which is their shared possession; and, on the other hand, to contribute this possession to the whole enterprise of integrating a global community of nations. This double purpose corresponds perfectly to the highest morality of international relations. That morality does not demand the sacrifice of any parochial value to the "general welfare," but rather the effort to find the point of concurrence between the particular and the general value. The double purpose of the NATO nations fits into this standard of international morality on both the strategic and the spiritual level. On the strategic level, the defense of the North Atlantic community is not bought at the price of endangering world peace. It helps to preserve world peace, for it is obvious that if Europe were overrun by the forces of tyranny, that would be the beginning of a universal war. Strategically, NATO works within the policy of what has been defined as "containment." It does not threaten any of the satellite nations by any military measures. Its purpose is clearly limited to defense. But the defense of the seedpot of Western civilization is clearly also a defense against universal war.

The moral and spiritual purposes of NATO correspond to the highest norm of international morality equally well. For the issue in the global community is not only to avoid war but to promote the unification of the global community in terms which allow the several nations and diverse cultures to express their vital impulses and protect their cherished values in liberty. The tyranny which threatens them is informed by a simple utopian creed, according to which it is possible, and even desirable, to unify the whole of human society upon the basis of a new and pretentious secular religion, interpreted by a chosen elite and giving itself to the illusion that peace will follow upon the triumph of the "social forces" which are marked by its peculiar historical logic to bring peace to the whole community through their triumph. We have abundant evidence that these dreams of "peace" turn inevitably into a nightmare of tyranny because the creed envisages a monopoly of power for an "elite" class, at present represented by an "elite" nation. It is certainly one of the ironies of history that the tyrannical solution for the problem of community should have presented itself in a guise considered so plausible by the peoples which have only recently emerged from "colonial" control and from feudal-agrarian forms. The seeming plausibility of this implausible solution for the problem of community is one of the great hazards to peace in the non-industrial nations of Asia.

The European nations, on the other hand, have had the experience of substituting delicate balances of social forces to preserve justice within a domestic economy, and of allowing diversity of culture within the spiritual life of individual nations. They may justly claim therefore that they have evolved a tolerable answer to the problem of community—justice and freedom within their several national communities; that they are applying this answer to their common life as members of an Atlantic community; and that they regard both their several national experiences and their common experience as a laboratory for the achievement of community on a world scale. For the nascent world community is no doubt more diverse culturally than any national community; and it requires the solution which the Western nations have evolved more desperately than does any parochial community.

It is therefore not too pretentious a claim that the nations which share the treasures of "Western civilization" have a right and duty to preserve these treasures and to make them available to the world community. It is necessary to do this, if the non-technical part of the world community is not to fall into a tyrannically organized uniformity as it emerges from the uniformities of traditional organic agrarian societies. It must be confessed that this task is complicated by the fact that the agrarian non-technical nations have such lively and resentful memories of the impact of technical power upon their lives that they are often unable to realize the genuine virtues of Western nations, because they see those nations only with eyes colored by past resentments. These resentments are exploited by the Communists, who try to appear as "liberators" to people who want to be free and are not able to understand the new "imperialism" and the tremendous power lusts of their "liberators." Thus they are in danger of being subjugated by more cruel masters as they try to win, or to celebrate, their emancipation from the Western nations, who frequently exploited their technical superiority in their relation to the "weaker" nations. (These nations were "weak" only in the technical means of production.)

This past history complicates the problem of making the genuine treasures of Western civilization available to the world community. It proves moreover that the defense of Western civilization is only one, and not the only, problem which confronts a world community threatened by tyranny. It shows how necessary it is to integrate the task of the defense of Western civilization to the larger problem of saving the world community from tyranny. Fortunately this integration, which is not the immediate problem of NATO, is being accomplished with some vigor by the same nations which have banded together for the defense of their civilization. If they do not neglect this task and sincerely strive to dissipate historic resentments against their power, they cannot now be accused of desiring anything for themselves which they are not ready to share with the world. Nations and communities of nations are fortunate when they are so placed that, by defending their own liberties, they also contribute to the liberties of others not in their community of destiny. The NATO nations are in that fortunate position.

The Meaning of Labor Unity

[*The New Leader,* Vol. 38 (March 28, 1955), pp. 8–9.] Critical of Henry Ford's treatment of his workers in the 1920s, before Detroit's automobile industry was unionized by the CIO under the aegis of New Deal legislation, Niebuhr vividly appreciated the role of labor unions in modern society. When the CIO merged with the older AFL in 1955, he reflected on the event.

THE recent merger agreement between the AFL and the CIO closed another chapter of a decade and a half of social, economic, and political history. It may well be that these past fifteen years made the difference between the decadent capitalism of France, for instance, and the comparative health of our own.

The trade-union movement was not as strong a decade and a half ago as it is today. The right to organize and bargain collectively was still widely challenged, and labor lacked the power to stand up against the ever growing capital integrations in our economy. Without such power, it is difficult to see how a mass market for the ever growing productivity of our industry could have been maintained.

Then came the New Deal and the political encouragement of labor organization. Trade unions expanded. But their expansion was retarded by an organizational defect in the trade union movement. The workers who needed collective bargaining most were in the great mass-production industries. They were known as "semi-skilled." Their skills could be acquired without long apprenticeship. Therefore, the old craft unions were not suited for them. They needed a union of the industrial type, which could organize all the workers in the industry.

Perhaps it was a simple problem to devise a new type of organization for these workers. But the old craft unions could not achieve this task. I well remember the year 1926 when the AFL announced that it would organize the Detroit automotive industry. The Detroit Board of Commerce was scared at this gesture, but it proved to be only a gesture. The old craft unions were quite incapable of organizing the automotive industry. It required another decade to organize it under different auspices.

It isn't exactly ancient history, but some may have forgotten that the man who fashioned the instrument by which the mass production industries were organized was John L. Lewis. Lewis's monumental egotism does not make him a hero even in the labor movement, except perhaps among his miners. But in a free society all kinds of instruments are used for the achievement of justice. Certainly, Lewis gave the new organization the driving force required for its task.

It may also be remembered that John Lewis was not exactly scrupulous in the agents he picked for his organizational tasks. That is how the Communists infiltrated into the CIO; they were among the original organizers. It required a decade to rid the CIO of the Communists, but that task has been accomplished.

The new industrial unions were so successful in setting collective power against collective power, and the companies proved themselves, in the end, so flexible in coming to terms with the unions, that long-term contracts with escalator clauses, allowing for increased wages according to the price index, and an annual bonus for higher productivity are now established procedure.

These contracts represent the advance in our social history from the days when Ford workers were "laid off" every August for "retooling" and when they lost practically a year of work in the fateful year when the sales of the old Model T suddenly collapsed and the new Model A was not yet ready. They also represent an advance over the conditions when the "speed-up" in the Ford factories was notorious among the workers and stood in ironic contrast to Mr. Ford's worldwide reputation as a humanitarian. His grandson, with fewer pretensions, presides over a much more humane industrial process. But the humaneness is not so much the fruit of the character of one man as it is the consequence of a new social climate and of a better equilibrium of social forces, without which no society can attain justice.

The organization of the total union strength in one camp will raise the specter of "bigness" for the enemies of the union movement. But the danger, if any, of such a large organization to the democratic balance can be considered fairly only in the context of the larger problem of the bigness of social and economic units in our society generally. There is certainly less danger in balanced bigness than in unbalanced bigness.

At any rate, the development of the trade-union movement which was made possible by the two types of unions, craft and industrial, added to the forces and factors which have transmuted the social and political situation in America. We have moved from a situation in which American productivity threatened to destroy itself by its very inventiveness, to a comparatively secure, healthy economy and a new political climate. . . .

The significance of this development lies in the fact that the ideologies, with their pretensions of discerning a "logic" of history, were a source of confusion. On the other hand, the practical and spontaneous reaction to particular situations of injustice, and the invention of new social techniques for establishing social and economic equilibria, corrected injustices and gave our free society a health which made it immune to the Communist virus. The lesson to be learned is that the search for proximate goals of justice amid the complexities of a technical civilization is more important than the blueprints for utopia to which the sensitive spirits of a few decades ago were so much addicted.

Winston Churchill and Great Britain

[*Christianity and Crisis,* Vol. 15 (May 2, 1955), pp. 51–52.] When Churchill retired from public life at the age of eighty-one in April of 1955, Niebuhr reflected on his historical significance.

THE whole world, at least the entire democratic world, recognizes that with Sir Winston's retirement from his post as Prime Minister of Great Britain a political career of monumental proportions has come to its effective conclusion. It was a career that inspired not only a nation but a whole community of nations. Rarely has a man so gifted with every art and wisdom of statesmanship found his hour so providentially as when Churchill was called to the helm in Britain's and the world's darkest hour. He had not been in a position of real leadership through the long period between the two world wars. The disaster at Gallipoli seemed to have ended a very promising political career, not because he was responsible for the disaster but because the defeat of a project that he had planned gave a good pretext to his enemies to end the career of a brash young man whom many regarded as too ambitious and irresponsible for the delicate tasks of parliamentary leadership.

Hitler's triumphs and the free world's extremities gave him the chance to lead the nation and to establish the most interesting and inspiring example of a leadership that brought out the best in a people. Churchill possessed rare gifts of eloquence and courage, as well as strategic wisdom, which enabled a very hard-pressed nation to survive the bitter days of defeat that preceded the final victory over a very dangerous foe.

Churchill modestly declared recently that "it was given to me to provide the lion's roar and sometimes to direct the lion's claws to the right object, but the lion's heart was theirs," that is, the British people's. No doubt he was right. But who can say to what degree an eloquent and courageous statement of the innermost thoughts of a people may have fashioned the very thoughts themselves? There is such a circular relation between potentialities and actualizations, between the unformed will of a people and the forming of that will by a resolute and resourceful leader, that Churchill's estimate is probably much too modest. He was, at any rate, the very embodiment of all that is best in both the democratic tradition and in the Anglo-Saxon version of that tradition.

It may not be irrelevant to observe that even his eloquence (particularly in a day when most political leaders avail themselves of speech writers) had a very telling effect upon the temper and morale of the nation. His very eloquent "Blood, sweat and tears" challenge to the nation may not have made these prices of liberty easier to bear, but it gave a telling liturgical expression of the hard realities of the moment and dignified sacrifices that the people were prepared to bear.

When Churchill led the "Grand Alliance" to victory he seemed to have won enough glory for any one man. The British people evidently thought so, for in Churchill's words after the victory they "straightway dismissed me from leadership in their affairs." Indeed, there were great admirers of Churchill who declared rather facetiously that it would be good for Britain if Churchill "won the victory and died the next day of apoplexy." He was not supposed to have enough interest in economic matters, and probably did not have, to guide the nation through its postwar reconstruction. But Churchill confounded his friends and enemies by doggedly hanging on to his seat in Parliament and winning the next election over what seemed, only five years earlier, to be the Socialist "wave of the future" not only in Britain but in all Europe.

This victory has a social significance because it proved the British democracy capable of embracing and then rejecting the Socialist ideal, but rejecting it only in favor of a chastened Toryism that would solve the age-old problem of equality and liberty by espousing the equality that had become the moral and social ideal of the whole nation, but with a less doctrinaire equalitarianism than the Labor Party.

Whatever may be the social and political significance of Labor's initial triumph and subsequent defeat, the Tory triumph gave Winston Churchill another lease on power. This final chapter in his fabulous career gave him the chance to add to the laurels of statesmanship by proving that he possessed not only courage and eloquence but that rarest of all gifts among statesmen—prudence.

The Labor Party tried to scare the electorate by charges that Churchill was a "warmonger." He had warned the world of the Communist menace in the famous Fulton, Mo., speech. But he soon proved that, in an age which lived under the Damocles sword of atomic destruction, he could be as prudent as he was courageous in the Nazi days when he rallied the whole free world against a common danger.

He desired nothing so much as to gain the "last and dearest prize" of his life, that is, peace for a harassed world. He asked for a conference of the great nations "at the summit." He came to Washington a year ago and admonished our own rather inflexible nation that "we must have a real try at coexistence," particularly when mutual annihilation was the alternative and "the victor would survey the world in ruins." More recently he gave eloquent expression to the only hope that men may now cherish, and that is that the fear of annihilation may actually make for peace, contrary to all previous experiences with armament races. For, said he, we are living in a period in which "security is the child of terror, and survival is the twin brother of annihilation."

Churchill was forced by age to retire before he could win his life's "most cherished prize," but not before he could give proof that prudence as well as courage was among his great gifts as a statesman.

We have thus far considered Churchill's unique endowments as a statesman, conscious that his gifts are so great and unique that he will hold a very special place in the history both of his nation and of the democratic world. But we would not do justice to the whole subject if we did not consider Churchill as the typical product of the British culture and British traditions. His eloquence and courage may have formed, as well as expressed, the spirit of a people in their "finest hour." But the spirit of the nation also nurtured this man. He is its product. His eloquence is the fruit of the parliamentary tradition and his passion for free institutions is the expression of the long history of parliamentary democracy. The curious blend of aristocratic and democratic ideas is the very flower of the ethos of a nation that added the freedom of the bourgeois movement to the sense of the organic in a society maintained in the aristocratic tradition, and then added the equalitarian impulse of the working class movement to the libertarian impulse of middle class life.

Churchill is the product of the British genius for democratic government in another way. He could not have supplanted Chamberlain in the darkest hour of the nation's history without the flexibilities of parliamentary democracy, without the freedom of maneuver these institutions made possible.

His defeat at the end of the war must also be regarded as a triumph of democracy and as a part of the triumphant Churchill story, despite his bitter reflections at the moment.

No Tory government could have satisfied the national passion for "fair shares for all" nor tightened the belt of a war-impoverished nation as successfully as the Labor Government did. Furthermore, no Tory government could or would have engaged in the liquidation of empire that was made necessary, both by the weakness of the center of the empire and by the pent-up rebellion of the subject peoples, particularly in India. Churchill certainly could not have done it, for he was a romantic imperialist who prided himself on not being willing to remove a single star from "His Majesty's imperial diadem." These retreats were necessary for the health of both Britain and the world, and they could not have been possible without a shift in government, though Churchill was wise enough to accept the final retreat from Egypt, which he had originally opposed so strenuously.

In short, Churchill was saved by the virtues of parliamentary democracy from tainting the glories of his wartime leadership by exposing the residual weaknesses of his, and the Tory, outlook upon life in the days of retrenchment. Thus he was saved to return to power when it became apparent that the Socialist medicine could not of itself strengthen a war-impoverished nation, and that its failure to do so could not be remedied by a more consistent application of the Socialist medicine.

Thus the Churchill story gives us the most vivid picture of the creative interaction between a great personality and a nation. It confounds the theories of both those who interpret history in terms of the influence of its great personalities and those who minimize the power of personality and try to interpret it as the product of "social forces." Here we have a living and vivid display of the way personality and tradition interact in a healthy, free society. . . .

The Change in Russia

[*The New Leader,* Vol. 38 (October 3, 1955), pp. 18–19.] After Stalin died in 1953, Niebuhr saw hope that his successors and their bureaucracy did not share the fanatic belief, inherent in Marxist dogma, of inevitable war between the Communist and Western capitalist worlds.

EVERYONE is speculating on just how much the smile, which has replaced the scowl, on the Russian face may mean to us and our posterity. The pessimists are afraid that the Western world will be taken in by the smile. Indeed, there are indications that it has already strengthened the hands of the "neutralists," whether in India or in France, and that it will lead to a relaxation of the posture of alert defense which has contributed a good deal to the security of our present situation. Furthermore, the realists accurately point out that the "big thaw" in international relations has not brought a change in Communist behavior either in Germany or in Asia. It is, they warn, just one more evidence of Communism's tactical flexibility, of which we have had ample evidence in two decades. The overall strategy of Communism remains the attainment of world dominion.

The inconclusive bargaining with West Germany revealed clearly that Russia will not yield on such important issues as German reunification. The Communists evidently desire a detente very fervently, but they are trying to purchase it at a very cheap price.

These arguments are cogent as far as they go. It might be added that the "collective leadership" of Communism has merely restored the tactical flexibility which was one of Lenin's boasts and which was sacrificed in the later days of Stalinism, when Russian policy hardened into a hard and unimaginative intransigence. Furthermore, it must be recognized that this flexibility is more formidable and more difficult to counter than the old intransigence, which, incidentally, had the merit from our standpoint of covering many of our mistakes.

But this logic leaves one factor out of account. The original power of Communism derived from the combination of absolute fanaticism and tactical flexibility, which was Lenin's real contribution to the Communist cause. Lenin did not, of course, originate the fanaticism. That was inherent in the whole Marxist dogma, with its simple distinctions between exploited and exploiter, its too-simple conception of the class structure of society, its too-simple derivation of all social evil from the institution of property, and its consequent division of every nation and of the whole world into friends and enemies "of the people." It was this fanaticism which enabled Lenin to organize a minority of the revolutionary forces in Russia into an integral political power which was able to dominate first the revolutionary cause, then the whole nation.

Lenin did combine tactical flexibility with this fanaticism, and the combination proved very successful in the early days of Communism. Stalinism boasted considerable flexibility in its day, enough to outrage the moral sense of mankind when, for instance, Stalin made his deal with Nazism. But the flexibility never dissolved the fanaticism. Thus, we could be allies of the Russians during the war, but it was not long before we were held up to scorn as "imperialists," "militarists" and "warmongers." The world was sharply divided once more, according to Communist dogma, into the hosts of good and evil. Every "capitalist" nation was as evil as the capitalist class, and every nation which stood on the other side of the revolution was "peace-loving" and intent only on defending itself against the "warmongers."

It is this fanaticism which is in prospect of being dissolved by Communism's new tactical line, and the prospect is the most hopeful development in contemporary history. When the party boss, Nikita Khrushchev, asserted after Geneva that "both sides are now convinced that neither side wants war," he may have written the close of a chapter in Communist history. We are no longer "warmongers." Capitalism is not intrinsically related to "imperialism," and the world is no longer divided between good and evil nations and classes. Chinese Premier Chou En-lai may still naively believe that the "ruling circles" in Wall Street meet every morning to send down their orders to Washington, but the more sophisticated Soviet bureaucracy does not have this simple picture of a complex world. As the complexities of the political scene begin to penetrate through the dogmatic preconceptions, empirical reality is bound to dissolve the fanaticism which gave the Communist world its cohesion and its striking power.

If this should be a significant development, the exchange visits of farm experts between Russia and America may well prove to be as important as the Geneva Conference. If the Russian farm experts still adhered to the dogmatic Communist picture of our world, they must certainly have been disillusioned when they investigated the lush farms of Iowa and other Midwestern states. They could not possibly fit these prosperous farmers into the category of the "exploited."

Stalin was probably right in sensing that the dogmas of Communism could be maintained inviolate only by rigorously prohibiting a commerce of ideas between the two worlds. The current Russian bosses have embarked upon the adventure of reducing the height of the Iron Curtain, and they have thereby imperiled the fanatical basis of Communist power. Their present policy may be more formidable than the previous intransigence, but it is certainly not immediately as dangerous to the peace of the world. Certainly the danger of being involved in war, because the Communist oligarchs believed their own propaganda and therefore misjudged their foes, has been at least partially eliminated.

If we may hope for the dissolution of the spirit of fanaticism, this hope does not include the disintegration of the Communist dogmatic base. Historical analogies suggest that the dogmas will be preserved for a long time after the fanatical fury of the dogmatism has disappeared. The most persuasive historical analogy is the political course of the Islamic movement. Moslem power was consolidated in the Middle Ages and threatened the whole of Christendom much as Communist power threatens Western civilization today. Its conception of a necessary "holy war" against all infidels was analogous to the Communist conception of the inevitable conflict between capitalism and Communism. The quasi-universalism of this Moslem power, transcending Arab nationalism while rooted in the Arabian world, is analogous to the relation between the pseudo-universalism of the

Communist creed and Russian nationalism. The rigorous equalitarianism of both creeds is similar even as the religious basis of political power is analogous. It must be understood that, while Communism is officially anti-religious, we may rightly speak of it as religious because it seeks ultimate ends, regarded as redemptive for the whole of mankind, by its political maneuvers.

At one point, the analogy breaks down. The dissolution of Moslem fanaticism did not occur until after it had involved the whole of Europe in war and had established its dominion over a considerable part of the Western world. But the inexactness of all historical analogies must not obscure the lessons which may be drawn from these analogies. The important fact is that Moslem fanaticism was gradually dissolved without any explicit disavowal of Moslem dogma. The complexities of history gradually made for dissolution of the fanaticism and the efficacy of the call for a "holy war." The Sultan of Turkey's effort to call for a holy war when Turkey became involved in World War I proved abortive; his failure marked the end of the threat of Islam to any established order. In current history, its power had disintegrated to such an extent that it was not even able to unite the Arab nations against the establishment of the new State of Israel.

We must expect the Communist dogma to be preserved, perhaps for ages to come, and the Communist oligarchs to pay lip service to it for many decades. Whether they are true believers or whether skepticism has corroded their souls may be politically irrelevant so long as they recognize that they cannot challenge the dogma upon which their political power rests.

But it is not politically irrelevant in the long run, for the corrosion of skepticism among both leaders and followers may prevent proclamation of the "holy war" which we have dreaded so much. In that sense, the "big thaw" may be one of the most important events of contemporary history. It may have ushered in a climate in which both a holy war by the Communists and precipitate action on our part to prevent a real or fancied holy war have become less probable.

It may be significant that more danger seems to arise in the present instance from Chinese rather than Russian Communism. The Chinese seem still to be true believers and to possess all the original fanaticism which is being dissolved in Russia. For all we know, the fear of becoming involved in a war initiated by the Chinese may have been a contributing cause of the "new look" which Russian policy has recently acquired. Whatever may be the truth about relations between the Russian and Chinese Communists, we cannot deny the fact that recent developments are quite different from what anyone could have predicted when we were in the winter of our discontent. These facts do not encourage complacency regarding the Communist menace, but they do throw a ray of promise into what was hitherto a very dark future for mankind.

Our Stake in the State of Israel

[*The New Republic*, Vol. 136 (February 4, 1957), pp. 9–12.] Sensitive to the plight of the Jews under Nazi tyranny, Niebuhr became a steadfast supporter of the Zionist cause during and after World War II. He wrote this article several years after the establishment of Israel in 1948.

THE tragic epic of the people of Hungary has so enthralled the imagination of the world that we are in danger of being indifferent to another drama of current history, which is invested with a peculiar pathos and which may end in tragedy because of our blindness.

To appreciate the full flavor of the drama of the state of Israel one must recount its history from the beginning, and even from the beginnings before its birth. The calendar beginning of Israel was the United Nations resolution, which sanctioned the new state, and the heroic battle which the nascent nation waged against the Arab nations, sworn to throttle Israel in its cradle. Thus the state's birth was both a gift from the world community and an achievement of the redoubtable army which the little nation was able to organize. It will be remembered that the Arab nations defeated in that conflict were then, as now, without unity or effective discipline, and that a young lieutenant of the Egyptian army, by the name of Nasser, was so moved by the shame of the defeat that he resolved on the overthrow of the corrupt Farouk monarchial regime, which symbolized the impotence of Egypt so perfectly.

But there were other beginnings before this calendar birth, without which the obvious beginning would not be explicable. Among those there was the dream of the young Jewish intellectual, turned Zionist, Theodore Herzl, who conceived of a homeland for a homeless nation; and the dream of a British Jewish scientist, Chaim Weizmann, who persuaded a reluctant British Government, holding a mandate in Palestine, to commit itself after World War I to the Balfour Declaration which promised to provide a "homeland" for the Jews in Palestine. Nationhood was not promised, but the declaration permitted a more generous Jewish immigration to Palestine though the rate of immigration was a constant source of friction between the Jews and Britain. The British naturally hoped to contain the Jewish homeland within the bounds of their imperial system and to guard the rights of the indigenous Arabs in a bi-national state. Indeed there were religious, rather than political, Zionists who thought that such a state would furnish the best solution for the problem of justice between Jews and Arabs. The famed Jewish philosopher, Martin Buber, and the late rector of the Hebrew University, Judah Magnus, were proponents of this plan, though it was probably unrealistic to expect an Arab majority gradually to accept a minority status, particularly when its loyalty would be divided between the pull of kinship and the pull of traditional homeland in Palestine.

Actually this modus vivendi was overwhelmed by the events which followed in the wake of the catastrophic fate of the Jews in the Nazi period. One hopes that the nascent anti-Semitism of the present period will be somewhat assuaged by a remembrance of these events, by a reminder of the fact that millions of Jews perished in the gas ovens and concentration camps of Hitler's Germany, and that the remnant found the continued insecurity of a corrupt Europe intolerable. Jewish immigration flooded Palestine and the uneasy conscience of the world as a result of the Nazi atrocities, and the humanitarian interest in finding security for the Jews of Europe, together with the sheer necessity of the Jews, created political forces which finally resulted in invalidating the British mandate, in prompting the United Nations to grant statehood to the nascent nation, and in assuring the new country of the passive sympathy of the non-Jewish world and the active sympathy of the Jews of the world, particularly the most numerous and prosperous Jewry of the United States.

Since then the new state has opened its doors to Jews from all over the world, has integrated them into a new community, whether they be from the backward culture of Yemen or the most advanced European cultures. It brought the most advanced techniques into the service of the new community, irrigated deserts in order to create orange groves and built a healthy industrial life through the skills of its people. Of course these miracles of integration and creativity would not have been possible without the continued financial support of world Jewry and particularly of the Jews of America, though critics who emphasize this fact usually do not consider that the oil royalties which flow into the Arab states exceed in value even these generous subsidies. But only a trickle of this oil wealth is used for raising the miserable standards of these moribund Islamic nations.

The history of the new state of Israel is thrilling in many respects. It represents a remarkable co-operation of "capitalistic" European and American Jews with the essentially socialist Jews of Israel. For the prevailing political ideology of Israel was determined by the Polish Jewish socialists, turned Zionists, so completely typified by the robust Prime Minister of today, Ben-Gurion. The collective farms or "kibbutzim" are, in fact, based upon rather doctrinaire socialist principles of the 19th Century, and are probably too consistently collectivist in their attitude toward family life to satisfy our robust individualism. A witty Jewish Oxford don, a friend of Chaim Weizmann, has given it as his opinion that Israel is served by the German Jews, who become honest and skillful "bureaucrats" and scientists, and by the Polish Jews who furnish the ideology and the political skill of the new state. Certainly the effective leadership of the state is divided between the German and the Polish Jews.

The co-operation between the religious Jews and the essentially secular idealists in the new state is equally worthy of note. Zionism is a political dream of religious origin, and before the Nazi period it was nourished only among those who were poor and orthodox, rather than among the "liberal" and assimilated and prosperous Jews. Hitler's persecutions changed all this and made Zionism popular in the congregations of liberal Judaism. From a religious standpoint one might say that it became too popular because the liberal rabbis were as preoccupied with Hitler for two decades as they are now with Nasser, so that even a Christian, with sympathies for Zionism, such as the present writer, can appreciate the protests of the anti-Zionist "Council for Judaism," which believes that political and nationalistic preoccupations of the rabbis imperil the religious substance of Judaism as a monotheistic faith.

It is a fact, however, that liberal versions of Judaism have found no lodging place in the new state of Israel. The religious Jews are orthodox and to such a degree that, if they would have their way, they would fasten upon this essentially secular community political standards directly derived from the book of Deuteronomy, which would, among other embarrassments, make the life of a modern woman intolerable. During the meeting of the World Council of Churches, held in Amsterdam in 1948, one of the members of the council was approached by an orthodox rabbi from Jerusalem with the suggestion that the religious Jews of Israel would like the support of Christians for their effort to create a religious state. He was very much surprised to be told that this Protestant assembly had just condemned religious political parties, that it avowed secular politics for the sake of religious principles and that it abhorred a sacerdotal state.

It is as a matter of fact one of the marvels of the new state that a religious party (informed by an archaic piety) and a secular party (informed by a rather self-conscious secular enlightenment) could co-operate in building the new nation. This miracle can only be explained by the force of the overarching national loyalty, the different interpretations which Ben-Gurion and the orthodox rabbis place upon the traditional liturgies and festivals of the Jewish faith, which are undoubtedly religious but are susceptible to political and cultural interpretations. A shrewd Israeli journalist informed the present writer that the chasm between the two groups prompted abandonment of the plan of writing a constitution for the new state. It was a wise move because the chasm could not have been bridged by any legal arrangement but only by the pressures and creativities of actual history. It must be counted as one of the achievements of American liberal religious Jews that they have not allowed either the doctrinaire secularism or the archaic religion to dampen the ardor of their support of Israel.

In any event it is apparent that no nation has ever come into being through a confluence of so many political and cultural and religious factors as this new state. The economic and spiritual investments in it by the West are very great. So also is our strategic stake. For Israel is the only sure strategic anchor of the democratic world, particularly since Khrushchev and Nasser have proved that Islam is not as immune to Communism as had been supposed, but is, rather, an almost ideal ground for the growth of nationalism posing as Communism and Communism posing as nationalism.

The question for us is how we can save the state from annihilation, for it is still the sworn intent not only of Nasser but of the whole Arab world to destroy it. There is in fact a real pathos in the fact that the Jews should have exchanged the insecurity of Europe for the collective insecurity of the Middle East. The West did not reckon with the depth of the Arab spirit of vengeance, nor did it appreciate that this technically efficient democracy would exacerbate the ancient feud between the Jews and the Arabs. For Israel is an offense to the Arab world for three reasons:

1. It has claimed by conquest what the Arabs regard as their soil; and Denis Brogan may be right (*NR*, Dec. 17, 1956) in declaring that this is one modern state which has been brought into being by force of arms. The West and the Jews may claim the previous Jewish right to the soil of Palestine, but we tend to forget that this right evaporated some thousands of years ago and that the Arabs are not impressed by the prophecies of the Old Testament, at least not by the political relevance of these prophecies. So strong is this Arab feeling that no Arab leader has yet promised to confer with Israel directly about any mutual problem.

2. This enmity has been increased by the problem of the refugees whom the Arab states will not resettle and whom the Jews cannot absorb except in small numbers without imperiling the security of their nation, because the refugees are sworn enemies of the new state. I do not pretend to judge between the Arab claims that they were driven out and the Jewish claims that they fled or were called out during the war. Both claims may be partially true or true in some sense. The point is that the refugees are a constant source of anti-Israel animus in the region.

3. The third cause of trouble is even more potent. The state of Israel is, by its very technical efficiency and democratic justice, a source of danger to the moribund feudal or pastoral economics and monarchical political forms of the Islamic world and a threat to the rich overlords of desperately poor peasants of the Middle East. It is also a threat to those Islamic religious people who delight in the

"organic" quality of this ancient life and who know that modern techniques would certainly destroy the old way of life in the process of lifting the burden of the poor.

The sources of enmity are in fact so many that it is idle to expect to pacify the region by even the most ambitious plan for the development of the economic resources of the whole region. All such proposals do not gauge the depth and the breadth of the Arab spirit of vengeance correctly. It is of such proportions that even an erstwhile pro-Zionist may be permitted to doubt whether it was right for the Western world to push its unsolved problem upon the Middle East where there was so much tinder for conflagration. Zionism was, of course, unthinkable without the original religious impetus, even though the statesmanlike achievements of the modern state are purely secular. But perhaps these qualms are irrelevant, for it is not possible to roll history back, and it has been proved that we cannot wean the Arabs from their passions by equivocation in regard to Israel.

The simple fact is that all schemes for political appeasement and economic cooperation must fail unless there is an unequivocal voice from us that we will not allow the state to be annihilated and that we will not judge its desperate efforts to gain some strategic security (by holding on to the Gaza Strip and demanding access to the Gulf of Aqaba, for instance) as an illegitimate use of force. . . .

The location of the state of Israel may have been a mistake; though the confluence of historical forces made it unavoidable. The birth and growth of the nation is a glorious spiritual and political achievement. Its continued existence may require detailed economic strategies for the whole region and policies for the resettlement of the Arab refugees. But the primary condition of its existence is our word that we will not allow "any nation so conceived and so dedicated to perish from the earth."

Tragedy in South Africa

[*The Messenger*, Vol. 22 (September 3, 1957), p. 5.] During the 1950s, South Africa's governing white minority imposed on the nation's black majority the most rigid policy of racial segregation in the world, known as apartheid—a system dismantled in the early 1990s. Niebuhr here commented perceptively and presciently on the situation.

THE news that all but the Dutch Reformed Church in South Africa—that is to say, the Roman Catholic, Anglican, Methodist, and Congregational churches—are prepared to defy the government's new law enjoining segregation on the churches, throws a vivid light upon the whole South African situation. It reveals all of the facets of the South African tragedy in one act.

A part of the tragedy is that the government, which has dared to decree this absurd law extending the logic of *Apartheid*—that is, rigorous segregation of the races—so that the churches are included, is, in effect, a "Christian" government; or, more precisely, it is the Dutch Reformed Church in its political activity. The most effective representatives of the government are ministers of the Dutch Reformed Church and the former prime minister, Daniel Malan, a theologically trained pastor. The "Nationalist" party is, in effect, the Dutch party.

It is this Christian party which has made the lot of the Negro progressively worse by its insistence on rigorous segregation, first in housing, then in schools, and now in the churches. The racist fanaticism, prompted by the fear of losing the identity of a European culture in an amalgam of the races, has reached the point where even the orthodox Christian universalism, based on the Pauline assertion "in Christ there is neither Jew nor Greek, neither bond nor free," is negated.

A second aspect of the tragedy is that one of the contributing factors to this fanatic racist attitude of the Dutch farmers is derived from their sense of inferiority toward the English part of the South African culture. The Dutch are farmers, and the English are in control of much of the business of South Africa, particularly the diamond, gold, and uranium mines. This sense of inferiority has made any common Christian witness impossible. In this respect, the South African situation is analogous to our Deep South where a Christian witness is discredited if it happens to be made by a "Yankee." It is, therefore, not certain whether the defiance of the churches will move the government. They are "English" churches, and the conflict between the English and the Dutch complicates the whole racial situation.

The third aspect of the tragedy is that this absolute defiance was occasioned only by the government's effort to violate the sanctity of the church as a community of grace rather than a community of race. . . . But who are we to criticize? Our churches have been segregated for generations, not by law, but by custom. With us, it was the civil state which challenged the custom, whereas in South Africa the state raised the custom to the dignity of law and prompted the Christian rebellion.

Fortunately, the extremism of the government has shocked even the Dutch Reformed Church and has encouraged a little group of dissidents, chiefly professors in their theological seminary, who have long been critical of the Christian racism of the church and government. Knowledgeable observers believe that any leaven in the Dutch community is worth twice any measure of leaven among the English-speaking people. The English mine the diamonds and the gold, but the Dutch preside over the political destinies of South Africa.

Coexistence under a Nuclear Stalemate

[*Christianity and Crisis,* Vol. 19 (September 21, 1959), pp. 121–22.]

THE most obvious condition of our existence is the nuclear balance of terror. Each side has enough of the dreaded weapons to make the difference between victory and defeat irrelevant and to make it imperative for the whole world that a nuclear war be prevented. There is little prospect of reducing any general war to non-nuclear proportions. Efforts at nuclear disarmament will undoubtedly continue but with small prospect of success since every disarmament conference is bound to deal with the whole balance of power between the contestants and not merely with nuclear weapons.

The peace is bound to be precarious because it depends upon preserving a fairly even balance of nuclear weapons, for a serious imbalance would tempt the stronger side to make demands that might result in hysteria on the part of the weaker side. No such situation has ever before existed in the history of the world. Mankind is fated to exist under the threat of a "last judgment" created by the ingenuity of human inventiveness and the advance of modern science.

The second condition of our coexistence is that only a nuclear war is ruled out, while all the inevitable power rivalries that have existed since the beginning of history continue. The hazards created by a struggle between power blocs would be severe even if the blocs represented similar cultures, but now the world is divided between two categories of forces under Russian and American hegemony.

The one alliance is dominated by an ideology that has formed a new civilization, appealing particularly to the technically backward nations of the world to whom it offers quick industrialization. It also has many characteristics of a democratic society, particularly in the realm of education where it is the custom of Communist society to relate opportunities to talent without reference to birth.

We have too long thought of communism in terms of analogy with the moribund autocracies of the past in which there was no social mobility. The Communist civilization must develop hierarchies of authority and power that stand in strong contrast to its early equalitarian creed. But it will produce a social mobility that will engage the loyalty and enthusiasm of its youth. We must expect it to be immensely attractive to the peoples of Asia and Africa, though it will be deficient in the virtues of the "open society" that has gradually developed by a tortuous process in the West and can hardly be duplicated in the rest of the world.

The third condition of coexistence is most relevant to American interests, for it involves the effective hegemony of our own nation in the non-Communist world. This hegemony offers some real hazards since we are probably too technocratic and too interested in high living standards that will seem vulgar to the poor nations ambitious to escape the deprivations of agrarian poverty. Furthermore the equilibrium of social forces that has made liberty compatible with both justice and stability is beyond the immediate reach of the nascent nations. They can more easily slip from traditional collectivism to technically efficient collectivism; they may regard our democracy not as a necessity but a luxury.

Freedom of spirit is a necessity in a genuinely humanistic culture. But [democracy is] a luxury that can be afforded only by nations that have achieved that equilibrium of social forces upon which justice depends, nations that have cultural and economic mutualities strong enough to bind the community into a unity so that political liberty may be hazarded. It is this aspect of freedom, so dear to the West, that may seem so irrelevant to many of the nascent nations. After all many of the nations in the non-Communist world are military or other dictatorships.

President Eisenhower's project for an exchange of visits with Premier Khrushchev is undoubtedly hazardous, but it must be credited to the President's courage and ingenuity that he is willing to hazard this in light of the complete diplomatic impasse. He is undertaking to build, in effect, a bridge of understanding across a political chasm on which no diplomatic bridge could be built—witness the failure to reach a disarmament agreement and the even graver failure to reach an accord on Berlin and East Germany. This means that we have despaired of any short-range results and are therefore undertaking to create some long-range results in understanding.

The project is commendable because the misunderstandings between the two hegemonous powers are very great. Russia looks at us through the myopia of the Marxist dogma; it judges us in terms of the social and political facts that obtained in the capitalism of the nineteenth century. Khrushchev, who has leavened the lump of Marxist dogmatism with a fair grasp of the empirical realities, still mouths the Marxist slogans against capitalism. He may still be too much the dogmatist to realize the true nature of our realities. Nevertheless, his visit will be a window through which Russian journalists may see and report the actual facts about American capitalism and democracy. His visit may contribute something to a relaxation of those dimensions of the tensions that are due to ideological distortions.

On the other hand we also have some serious misconceptions of Russian life. They arose from Stalinist despotism, which persuaded all or most of us to regard communism as a pure distortion of the Marxist utopian dream. Russia under the post-Stalin oligarchy is not a democracy and may never be. But there are dynamic and creative elements in Russian civilization to which we are, if blind, blind to our peril. Among them is an educational system that offers a fair equality of opportunity to talented youth in a technically advancing civilization that bids fair to match our own and to surpass it in some instances. This remains true even if Mr. K.'s boasts are extravagant. We are not dealing with a new version of czarist despotism. That old analogy, so polemically popular, does not describe any of the essential facts in the present Russian scene. . . . The remaining tension is a part of the price we must pay for living in the most hazardous period of history and for being one of the two great "imperial" powers in this period.

Imperialism in Perspective

[*The New Leader,* Vol. 41 (November 14, 1960), pp. 7–8.] As the movement in Africa for national independence spread to Nigeria and the Congo (now Zaire) in 1960, Niebuhr reflected that, where the Belgians had failed, the British proved the creative values of imperial rule.

THE tragic history of the Congo Republic, set free before it was ripe for self-government, is a reminder to both the free and the Communist world that modern imperialism, or in fact imperialism as we have known it throughout human history, is *not* purely exploitative. It has its exploitative features. All relations of strength to weakness are partly exploitative; even the relation of parents to their children, though informed by love, may become exploitative. But imperialism usually has three motives:

- The missionary motive, the desire to confer the benefits of civilization on a backward culture. In more recent history the missionary motive has expressed itself in the impulse to bestow both the benefits of democratic political forms, and competent management of a technical and industrial economy (which the new nations desire almost as much as political freedom). All the new nations desire national independence with an almost universal yearning. Their resentment against the colonial powers is prompted not so much by economic exploitation, as the Communists believe, but by the racial arrogance characteristic of the imperial masters.
- The political motive, the desire for "power and glory." Winston Churchill's type of imperialism was dominated by the political motive. Luckily, the Conservative party was defeated by the Labor party just soon enough to grant India its independence. Churchill, though the greatest statesman of our age, had a romantic preoccupation with the glory of empire and was reluctant to give independence to India. He said he would not want to "remove a single jewel from His Majesty's crown."

- The economic motive, which I mention last not because it must be regarded the least powerful motive, but because it is not as powerful as the anti-imperialists believed.

These three imperial motives are variously mixed in all imperial ventures. Take the Congo tragedy. Anti-imperialists regard it as a telling revelation of exploitation. But if one compares the Congo with Ghana and Nigeria, the lesson is that good imperialism represents tutelage in the arts of self-government. The Congo was once the private domain of the King of Belgium and the older ones of us will remember the shocked reactions of the world to Congo atrocities. The Belgian Parliament took over direction of the African colony from the King as a result of the reactions in the democratic world.

The Belgians prided themselves on giving the Congolese the highest living standards in Africa. They ran the whole colony with a Belgian bureaucracy, and tried to settle the race problem by not allowing Belgians to gain property in the Congo. But the Belgians miscalculated in regarding the Congolese as children who, if they ate well, would not desire independence for decades to come. They gave them technical education for manning their rich copper mines and other tasks of modern industry, but they did not educate doctors, nurses or any administrative personnel necessary to man the political machine. The Congo had only a handful of university graduates on the day of independence compared with the thousands in Nigeria. Above all, the Belgians gave the Congolese no practical experience in self-government.

The Congolese colony was governed by the trinity of the copper interests, the colonial office and the church. The Catholic church was the most liberal of these three governing bodies. It had an uneasy conscience about imperialism, and therefore printed nationalist pamphlets on its presses, and it also realized that it would take time to prepare these primitive people for self-government. They would have to be trained first as technicians and then finally as mature, politically competent members of a self-governing nation. But the fires of nationalism, fanning over Africa, disturbed the tempo of this timetable. Riots broke out, warning the Belgians about their miscalculations.

Resentment against the white man's arrogance motivated this nationalism more than resentment against economic exploitation. Of course, the copper interests in Belgium profited from the colony. But the Congolese also profited from the mines, which they could not have worked by themselves. That has always been the relation of a technically advanced nation to a backward people.

It is easy to criticize the Belgians for their precipitate flight from the colony once political passions had been aroused. Their mistake was not so much in their flight—for you cannot mine copper any more than coal with bayonets—but in the arrogance which prompted their timetable for independence. The chaos which followed withdrawal of Belgian power proves how much an imperial frame of order is necessary in a culture which has political loyalties no higher than the tribal level and is incapable of furnishing its own cement of political cohesion. It also reveals that all foreign domination, however necessary, is grievous to the dominated. Every imperial power must therefore prepare its colonies for self-government as quickly as possible, particularly in the 20th century and particularly in an Africa aroused by the twin political passions of pan-Africanism and nationalism.

The Belgians, having failed in the task of cultural and political tutelage, thus launched a nation on the perilous path of self-government and confronted the world with a politically premature birth. The new nation promptly fell apart. Tribal and regional conflicts spread chaos and bloodshed in the once peaceful region. The new "constitution" did not work, for constitutions are not self-supporting. What was the "authority" of the new President Joseph Kasavubu? He was the head of a small party, which believed—wisely, as it turned out—in a federation of the various regions, but he was defeated by the Premier, the ineffable Patrice Lumumba, who was against federation and in favor of a strong central government. But the strong central government could not command the loyalty of either the Army or the provinces—particularly copper-rich Katanga Province—which preferred to have order with the help of the Belgians rather than be immersed in the chaos of an incompetent political leadership. . . .

Meanwhile the greatest midwife of new nations, Great Britain, having given Ghana its independence three years ago, has now launched the potentially greatest nation of Africa, Nigeria, on the sea of national liberty. These two former African colonies prove that the missionary motive, or at least the creative function, of imperialism is not illusory. Both Ghana and Nigeria have a higher culture and competence than Liberia, that old independent African nation, in which some ex-slaves from America have preserved an uncreative oligarchy under constitutional forms for over a century without much progress.

But even these well-prepared new nations, Ghana and Nigeria, will have problems of preserving stability and justice and, above all, national unity against regional and tribal loyalties. In Ghana the redoubtable Kwame Nkrumah, while paying lip service to the constitutional forms and parliamentary urbanities of his British tutors, has created a one-party state, probably under the force of necessity, for only the urban population of the former Gold Coast is thoroughly imbued with patriotism.

In Nigeria, the colonial masterpiece of the late Lord Luggard, the three regional Governments are not thoroughly cemented. The northern region is both backward and socially integrated under its Islamic Emirs. The two other regions are partly Christian and partly cultural and religiously primitive. Tribalism, nationalism and pan-Africanism will weave their complex patterns of history on the African continent for centuries to come. The advanced nations can help them solve their problems, though the days of explicit tutelage are over, but they really have their own destiny in their own hands. Their history is not likely to be less dramatic, confused and complex than was the history of the European nations from the 16th to the 19th centuries.

The Mounting Racial Crisis

[*Christianity and Crisis,* Vol. 23 (July 8, 1963), pp. 121–22.] Niebuhr wrote this piece after the movement led by Martin Luther King, Jr., encountered violent opposition in Birmingham, Alabama, and President Kennedy addressed the nation proposing legislation enacted a year later as the Civil Rights Act of 1964. The massive March on Washington, addressed by King, took place several weeks after this piece appeared.

THE simplest explanation for the increasingly urgent demonstrations of the Negroes against disfranchisement, segregation in school and church, lunch counter and public conveyance, and against every public custom that affronts the dignity of the human being, is that the Negro feels—as we all ought to feel—that a century is a long time to wait for the elimination of the "American dilemma."

Discriminations against a race in the present historical context are as offensive to the conscience of man and as unbearable to the victims of discrimination as slavery was in its day. If we recognize that the present situation is more unbearable to the victims of injustice than it is offensive to the conscience of men, we are confronted by the hardness of the human heart, even among those whose hearts have been softened by human sympathy and the stirrings of conscience. Try as we will we cannot feel the pain of others as vividly as they do.

If we should still find it a mystery that this burst of resentment has come in a period in which the ice of the long winter of injustice is breaking—after the Supreme Court decision on segregated schools has given unmistakable evidence that the law of the nation is now unequivocally on the side of justice and during an Administration that has shown more concern for racial justice than any previous one, despite the Southern base of the regnant party—we have only to consider that social revolt is not, as Marx thought, motivated by pure desperation. It is motivated by both resentments and hopes, particularly by hopes deferred, which "maketh the heart sick."

The Supreme Court had promised integrated schools "with all deliberate speed." Yet a decade has passed without obvious progress. The customs of the nation, the pride of the dominant race, its fear of competition from a race whose increasing education would refute the dogma of its innate inferiority have inhibited the attainment of justice.

Impatience is due in part to the fact that some Negroes have attained a college education. Thus there is now an articulate core to voice the longings of the voiceless masses. They have performed the same service for their race as the articulate craftsmen performed for the peasants at the birth of democracy in the 17th century. Moreover, they have given evidence, particularly in the realm of sports and the arts, in theater and concert hall, and in the novel that the vicious theory of their innate inferiority is a fraud. Their leaders in these fields have sparked the flame of the present revolt as much as the students did with their original sit-ins at the lunch counters and their Freedom Rides.

Since the record of the white Protestant Church, except for a few heroic spirits, is shameful, one must record with gratitude that Negro churchmen have been conspicuous among the leaders in the revolt. The Negro church in the person of Dr. Martin Luther King has validated itself in the life of the Negroes and of the nation.

The impatience of the Negro will not subside until the last vestiges of legal and customary inequality have been removed. Revolutions do not stop half way. The next step has been outlined by the President's new legislative program, which is the natural fruit of the increasing tension of what he has defined as our "moral crisis."

The legislative program as proposed seeks to outlaw discrimination in all private commercial ventures on the basis of the 14th amendment and the Interstate Commerce Clause of the Constitution. It will not pass without a great political struggle. If successful it might put the legislative capstone on the emancipation of the race. But the retreating white supremacists are increasingly desperate. Their murders, their police dogs and their terror have contributed as much to the mounting tension as the impatience of the Negroes. We are, in short, confronted with the ultimate, or at least penultimate, chapter in the long history of overcoming the "American dilemma."

Of course laws cannot finally change the recalcitrant. Their prejudices dictate customs that are at war with the explicit law of the land and the law that is written into the heart. These prejudices are, in the language of St. Paul, "another law in my members warring against the law of my mind." One can only hope that the Church will be more effective in restraining and transmuting these vagrant and recalcitrant passions of man than it has been in the past. The contribution of Roman Catholicism is another story.

We Protestants might begin the new chapter in our national life by contritely confessing that evangelical Christianity has failed to contribute significantly to the solution of the gravest social issue and evil that our nation has confronted since slavery.

John Fitzgerald Kennedy, 1917–1963

[*Christianity and Crisis,* Vol. 23 (December 9, 1963), p. 221.]

THE untimely death of President Kennedy by an assassin's bullet has aroused a depth and breadth of grief in the nation and the world that historians may well regard as unprecedented.

Three reasons may be offered for the dimension and universality of the sorrow. First, the assassination cut short the life of a singularly gifted young statesman while in the midst of a promising career. President Kennedy possessed a unique combination of gifts. He had a quick and searching intelligence combined with a rare degree of political shrewdness and personal and political courage.

Other Presidents have died in office, and three before him were assassinated. But most of them died when their essential work was done. This applies even to Lincoln, who led the nation through the Civil War and was murdered when victory was in sight. Franklin Roosevelt died in office after guiding the nation through a crucial period in its history. But Mr. Kennedy was the youngest of our Presidents. Seemingly destined to lead the country for eight years, he was cut down after less than three years.

A second reason for the dimension of the grief was the promising, but unfinished, character of his political leadership. President Kennedy proved his mettle in foreign policy at least twice. He had the courage to confront the Russians in Cuba when a nuclear war was threatened—and averted by a combination of boldness and prudence. On the other hand he was more dedicated to the tremendous task of avoiding nuclear catastrophe than any contemporary leader, and he courageously initiated the limited test-ban agreement, which may well go down in history as the beginning of a new era in the Cold War.

In domestic policy his greatest task was to lead the nation in what seemed a final chapter in solving the "American dilemma," the failure to grant Negro citizens equal justice and respect for their human dignity. President Kennedy did not initiate the Negro revolution—perhaps it was sparked by the Supreme Court decision of a decade ago; perhaps it was the spontaneous combustion of the century-old resentment of citizens defrauded of a freedom and justice supposedly inherent in the American dream. We do not know.

But we do know that the President, confronted with the revolt, did not vacillate or temporize. He gave the Negro citizens the full support of the Federal power and summoned the nation to solve what was indeed a "moral crisis." President Kennedy's name will be associated with various creative endeavors, but his stand on civil rights will certainly head the list. It is too early to say whether his untimely death will arrest the movement toward justice or whether it may be as important as his life in completing the unfinished business of restoring the nation's moral integrity.

A third reason for the universality of the grief beyond our national borders was President Kennedy's creative thrust in world affairs. The prestige of the nation as the leader of the non-Communist world increased the prestige and power of the American Presidency. We must view with gratitude the providential selection of this gifted leader to exercise that power, and we confront his death with an anxious and prayerful attitude about American world responsibilities in the future.

From Bad to Worse in Vietnam: Pretense and Power

[*The New Leader,* Vol. 48 (March 1, 1965), pp. 6–7.] Opposed through the 1950s to U.S. military involvement in the Vietnamese civil war, Niebuhr accepted during the early 1960s a limited American advisory role in support of South Vietnam's struggle against Communist insurgency. But he sharply criticized President Johnson's escalation of U.S. participation in February of 1965 by ordering the bombing of targets in North Vietnam, followed by growing American troop deployments.

FOLLOWING each of his periodic inspection trips to Vietnam, Secretary of Defense Robert McNamara returns home with assurances that the situation is improving there. The unhappy truth is, however, that matters have been going from bad to worse in Vietnam for years.

Walter Lippmann thinks we should never have permitted ourselves to become involved in the mess left behind by France's defeat in its Indochinese empire. But it is difficult to see how we could have avoided the responsibilities of our position as leader of the democratic world after former Premier Pierre

Mendes-France, at the 1954 Geneva Conference, withdrew France from the shambles of its defeat. All Mendes-France could obtain was the neutralization of two of the three little peasant nations of the peninsula; something still had to be done about Vietnam.

The Communist "liberator" of that nation, Ho Chi Minh, would naturally have conceded any solution, because all solutions seemed to give him the prestige of being the father of his nation's independence. But Vietnam contained a politically competent, anti-Communist Catholic minority which was understandably fearful of Ho's domination. The small nation was therefore divided, with many of the Catholics of the North fleeing to the non-Communist South—a situation that aggravated the anti-Catholic animus of the Buddhist peasants.

The Ngo family of Catholic mandarins was sufficiently anti-French to invest the struggle with the saving dignity of patriotism. One brother, Diem, ousted the French puppet emperor, Bao Dai, and organized a "democratic government." But the government made little impression on the peasants, who simply wanted to be left alone, and Diem's brother, the famous Madame Nhu's husband, proved remarkably resourceful at arousing personal animosities and brutally suppressing the Buddhists. Despite its democratic pretensions, moreover, the survival of the Diem regime depended upon the support of the Army, and the Diem government was eventually, and brutally, overthrown in an Army revolt.

Since the bloody fall of Diem, Army coups have followed each other with depressing regularity. While our ambassadors have attempted to persuade successive military juntas to adapt themselves to some semblance of civil government, their efforts have not been impressive—which may explain why McNamara has felt it necessary to tell us repeatedly that this continuing political turmoil is not seriously hindering the war against the Communists.

All the while, though, the Communist North has been increasingly successful at infiltrating the South, and has shown itself capable of organizing much more than guerrilla bands. When the Vietcong staged terror raids on South Vietnamese installations, we retaliated with air strikes against Northern military installations and supply depots. Our theory was that our resolution was being tested and it followed that we could not fail in the test. Our rigorous action had enthusiastic bipartisan support in Congress—though an increasing number of Congressmen seem apprehensive about the course of our whole involvement in France's former empire.

The retaliatory air strikes may indeed have proved our resolution. But in a military sense they showed only that we have superiority in the air—and thus at least a balance against increasing Communist superiority on the ground. In short, we seem clearly bogged down in a war which neither side can win.

General Lucius Clay may have been right in insisting that strategy and hegemonic prestige demand that we prove our determination not to be driven out of Southern Asia. Our strategic interests involve, after all, the rich monarchic nation of Thailand, governed by a tight military dictatorship, yet strongly anti-Communist. References to Thailand have been muted because the ideological veil of strategic interests demands that our leaders concentrate on the little "democracy" of South Vietnam, thus assuring the world that we would always come to the aid of nations struggling to "preserve their freedoms."

But evidence multiplies that the peasants of South Vietnam have not exactly been echoing Patrick Henry's cry, "Give me liberty or give me death!" They want merely to cultivate their rice paddies, and be at peace. They probably have regarded Catholic rulers with as much suspicion as they regard the Communists. To many peasants, Ho Chi Minh is the true liberator of the nation. Our ideological defense of the war has thus been less than plausible.

The strategic reason for our involvement makes more sense, at least to an inner circle of Vietnam's politically sophisticated citizens. But Secretary U Thant of the United Nations and a host of world leaders have called our strategic motives into question. Does it make sense to level the cities of both North and South, they ask, in a war which neither side can win? Would not a general conference on the crisis be preferable to continued carnage?

Of course, we have had some experience with these general conferences, beginning with the one in Geneva in 1954 that produced the unworkable solution of dividing Indochina in the first place. Notwithstanding past experience, however, it might now be the better part of wisdom to accept the proposition that our confrontations with Communist power, in this case Chinese Communist power, will result in our having to live with unsolved problems—whether in Berlin or Korea or Indochina. Our warlike stance may be prompted by strategic motives, but moral prestige is also a part of our authority, and that may be damaged irretrievably by our demonstrations of air superiority.

There is always the chance, too, that increased Sino-Soviet rivalry will work to our advantage in a general conference. Ho Chi Minh is one of the few Asian Communist bosses who is more loyal to Moscow than to Peking, probably because he fears the embrace of a very close, very powerful neighbor. No doubt the wily old gentleman could persuade Moscow to save his nation from Peking. Since our original purpose was to prevent Chinese power from expanding in Asia, a general conference might therefore work toward that end. Such an arrangement would always be vulnerable to a subsequent reconciliation between the two giant Communist nations. But that is one of the hazards we face in this curious triangular relationship.

Perhaps we could estimate the hazards more accurately if we stopped pretending that our only concern is for the liberty of that "democratic" government planted in the soil of a peasant society, a society left untended for decades by the French masters of the peninsula. (One measure of the dismal French colonial record is the fact that Vietnamese Buddhists and Catholics, if able to agree on nothing else, still share a bitter animus against the French—bitter enough to lend irony to de Gaulle's proffers of advice.) But we cannot afford to ignore the consciences of many of our devoted allies—and our own conscience as well—where bombing of the North is concerned, even if such raids are in retaliation for the cruelties of the enemy in the South.

In measuring the moral, political and strategic hazards of our Vietnamese policy, we should recognize that we are trying to manipulate China, one of the other two great super-powers whose might impinges on many of the nations of the world. We are not, as we sometimes pretend, an innocent idealistic nation helping a small nation preserve its freedom because we were once also the pawn of an empire. All our calculations, both in morals and politics, are confused by this devious, propagandistic pretension with which our embarrassed leaders seek to beguile us. We are a people not fully at home with the hazards of global politics, hazards which we face because our economic strength and nuclear capacity have lifted us up to the frightful position of leadership of the free world.

Adlai Stevenson: 1900–1965

[*Christianity and Crisis*, Vol. 25 (August 9, 1965), pp. 169–70.] Once governor of Illinois, Adlai Stevenson was the Democratic presidential candidate in 1952 and 1956 and served from 1961 to 1965 as U.S. ambassador to the United Nations. Niebuhr, whom he read and consulted and who twice supported him for president, here reflected on Stevenson's role in public life.

THE death of Adlai Stevenson in London forever stilled the voice, heart and mind of a statesman endowed with singular gifts. That voice had given the wings of rare eloquence, spiced with wit, to the spiritual and intellectual endowments of a leader who had meditated long and wisely on the problems raised by America's becoming a hegemonous power in a nuclear age, and on the domestic problems of a technological nation that had only recently come to terms with the requirements of justice in modern industry.

Adlai Stevenson could not present ultimate answers to the vexing problems of a powerful, but perplexed, nation. In fact, he was modest enough to suggest only proximate solutions. His modesty and his freedom from political clichés and grand slogans were characteristics that endeared him to thoughtful citizens, who had grown cynical about the sweeping promises of politicians. However, this modesty, as well as his wit, may have been handicaps in the political struggle, despite the favor in which the sophisticated held both attributes.

The fact that a man of such stature was twice defeated for the Presidency gives his career the flavor of pathos. As a candidate he won the solid affection of millions of Americans, and his popularity in Europe was phenomenal. The Europeans were so enthusiastic about Stevenson because they believed that urbanity and sophistication were lost virtues in American politics.

Yet he was twice beaten. His first defeat by General Eisenhower was, in a sense, inevitable. The nation's history is replete with the political success of war heroes, and the General won because he bore the laurels of military triumphs. Moreover Eisenhower was charmingly benign, amiable and decent. . . .

In Stevenson's second career as US Ambassador to the United Nations he made brilliant use of his endowments as a tribune not only of our nation but also of the hopes and yearnings of all the nations coming to birth. His sympathy for the underdeveloped cultures of the world was recently expressed with his usual clarity. He observed: "History gives us no warrant for the hope that desperately poor peoples will have permanent patience with the affluent ones."

Perhaps both the integrity and pathos of the career of this great man can best be shown by a comparison with a Roman Emperor. Marcus Aurelius was both Stoic philosopher and reigning emperor. As wielder of Roman power he was not conspicuously successful. But his humane wisdom nourished the civilized world for generations.

The depth and breadth of the grief over Adlai Stevenson's death may indicate a general awareness of men in all nations that we have parted not so much with a wielder of power as with a noble soul who prompted and expressed the highest aspirations of enlightened peoples.

Fighting an Intractable Dwarf

[*The New Leader,* Vol. 51 (August 5, 1968), pp. 12–13.] Niebuhr wrote a torrent of articles criticizing the massive U.S. military involvement in Vietnam during the Johnson and early Nixon years. This one appeared after American public opinion turned against the war, prompting Johnson not to seek another term and Nixon to run for office with the promise that he would get the nation out of Vietnam.

ONLY a quarter century after World War II, from which the U.S. and the U.S.S.R. emerged as imperial powers, we have stumbled into a futile civil war in a small nation. It seems incredible that the United States, with its vast resources for technological warfare, cannot win the Vietnam war, or at least negotiate an "honorable peace"—one, that is, that would enhance our political prestige in the world and particularly in Asia. After three months of formal and informal talks, the Paris peace conference is clearly deadlocked. It may well have more influence on the political conventions and Presidential elections in the United States than on the course of the war and the establishment of peace in Vietnam.

Indeed, it is quite probable that a dwarf nation like Vietnam is so intractable in accommodating a giant nation like the United States with an honorable peace because it shrewdly suspects the November elections will reveal that the giant nation is sick of this costly war, which the dwarf nation, fighting for Communist inspired "national liberation," is quite prepared to continue. We are, in fact, in the position of trying to frustrate the Communist formula for harnessing patriotism to the purposes of its ideology. The honorable peace we desire so fervently—and by which we hope to prove that a little sliver of a country with its capital in Saigon is really a viable democratic institution, even though it lacks almost every prerequisite of either integral community or democracy—is denied us because the Communists see our actions as merely an American substitute for the old French imperialism. . . .

Our Marshall Plan was so successful because it merely restored the industrial plant and communications destroyed by the War. Their own culture and history had furnished Western European nations with the social and technical presuppositions of a democratic order; and a common written language furnished the ethnic and linguistic bases for integral nationhood. Communism, on the other hand, appeared to us and to Western European nations in the guise of an "international conspiracy." Russia has since experienced difficulties in bringing nations such as Yugoslavia, Rumania and Czechoslovakia under the authority of its international system.

In Southeast Asia, however, we were confronted by colonial liberation and the fervor of Communist-inspired nationalism. Our ideology seemed irrelevant to the conditions of these former French colonies of Indochina. We sought to plant democracy in a peasant culture and succeeded only in creating the repressive Diem regime, which perished in a bloody military revolution. To the Vietnamese peasants Diem's government was merely a facade for the Catholic Mandarin landlords. Promised land reforms were ignored by Diem; and even now Rural Pacification, another name for land reform, has not been successful. The supposed integral nation was challenged for control of its own territory by the Communist Vietcong, which held many of the villages. Even now that the peace talks in Paris have begun, the Vietcong threatens Saigon with mortar destruction.

We attempted to give the military juntas ruling South Vietnam the dignity of constitutional integrity, of a "Charter" drawn up by a Constitutional Assembly. On the basis of this Charter elections were held, and President Johnson sent American observers to testify to their honesty. Lo and behold, two members of the junta were elected: Nguyen Van Thieu as President and former Premier Nguyen Cao Ky as Vice President. The runner-up in this election, Truong Dinh Dzu, was promptly jailed. . . .

We were drawn into the Vietnam quagmire by imperceptible stages. President Eisenhower was loath to offer military assistance, but did offer financial aid to the southern portion of the partitioned nation. By the time President Kennedy came to power Ngo Dinh Diem had established a kind of autocratic "Republic" by defeating the various Buddhist sects, and President Kennedy offered to provide him with military "consultants." After Diem and his brother Ngo Dinh Nhu were murdered, various Army juntas ruled South Vietnam with indifferent success.

The monstrous military expansion started under President Johnson, probably because of the sheer necessity of preventing our clients from suffering defeat at the hands of Hanoi. Obviously the military command suggested this military alternative to a defeat resulting from inadequate ideological, economic and political development in the South.

It is certainly a mystery why the shrewd politician in the White House, his native cunning sharpened by experience in Texas politics and years of Senatorial maneuvering, should have permitted this astronomical expansion of military effort, involving half a million soldiers and the fantastic financial cost of two billion dollars a month. Could he not have foreseen that the public would be disenchanted about this bloody and futile war, especially when its costs in blood and money were revealed? As the casualties began to rise to a total of 25,000 American dead and as the war made a 10 per cent tax surcharge necessary, it became clear that an otherwise successful Administration risked defeat in the November elections.

We must not forget the dwarf nation of North Vietnam in its encounter with the American giant. The Paris peace conference, deadlocked for months, will probably not reach a formula for an honorable peace until after the political conventions, at the earliest. The dwarf nation is thereby proving that, while it is unable to vanquish the giant, it does have the capacity to embarrass him and add to his store of wisdom in the first quarter century of his empire.

The Negro Minority and Its Fate in a Self-Righteous Nation

[*Social Action,* Vol. 35 (October 1968), pp. 53–64.] After passage of the Civil Rights Act of 1964 and the Voting Rights Act of 1965 ended legal inequalities of blacks and whites in the American South, most black Americans still lived under inherited economic disadvantages which, Niebuhr maintained, could only be overcome by government assistance in housing, education, and job training. In this piece he reviewed the whole problem after the Kerner Commission released its report on conditions in America's inner cities.

IN the summer of 1967 the poor, alienated, and resentful Negroes of the ghettos of our big cities erupted in violence. They burned, looted, and sniped and finally made a complacent white majority aware that it had awakened too late to meet the demands of this Negro minority. The riots occurred after the Supreme Court school integration decision of 1954 and the Civil Rights Act of 1964 had corrected the most obvious injustices from which the Negro minority suffered.

The President appointed a National Advisory Commission to investigate all the conditions which prompted the civil disorders. The Commission fortunately did not share the prejudices of the white racists. Instead, it recorded that the young Negroes were unemployed at a rate two and a half times that of white workers. The operation of an industrial culture made them not only unemployed but also unemployable, because they lacked the skill required by the technical operations of modern industry. The Commission was not puzzled by the arson and looting of the young Negroes. It established that there was a natural relation between narcotic addiction and crime and the unemployment of school dropouts.

The Commission recorded the various aspects of ghetto existence. The relationship of the Negro population to the police and the number of Negro police in various cities are faithfully recorded; the police incidents which sparked the riots are analyzed. The Commission also gives elaborate details of the education of young Negroes, the percentage of dropouts from high school and college. These statistics establish the fact that many Negroes are compelled by poverty to forego higher education or even, in some instances, primary education. For example, 17 percent of Negroes over 25 years of age are illiterate, and this is in an economy in which commercial services grow apace. Naturally, therefore, the Negro minority is at a disadvantage in getting white-collar jobs, as is illustrated by the low rate of Negro employment in the communications media.

In short, we have been given a full and fair report of the vicious circle of poverty, poor housing, unemployment, and underemployment. The comparison of median wage of Negro and white industrial workers reveals that the white earns more than twice as much as the Negro. And Negro unemployment runs at a rate of two and half times that of whites. In short, the Commission establishes the fact that our Negro minority is so deeply mired in poverty that it cannot escape without the help of government, and government of course represents the white majority.

The report of the National Advisory Commission on Civil Disorders clarifies many aspects of the tragedy of the relationship of the Negro minority to a complacent white culture. The Report neither condones the crime of these disorders nor accepts them as part of a genuine "Negro Revolution." Nor does it make the mistake of regarding these riots as the response of the Negro minority to the creative reforms of the national government for the correction of ancient wrongs. It merely records the historical facts which reveal that the riots were the response of poor Negroes, for whom the reforms came too late. Integrated schools and the right of suffrage might radically alter the place of the Negro minority in our American community, but the young unemployed and unemployable Negro was bound to express his alienation from our democracy by violence.

It is not, of course, the responsibility, nor is it within the competence, of this political committee to inquire about the reasons for the tardiness of this self-righteous nation in meeting so obvious a responsibility toward a minority which labors under two disadvantages: the dreadful burden of its slave past and its obvious divergence in physiognomy from the dominant white majority. It is, therefore, important for all of us who are interested in establishing a common humanity and equal civil rights for the Negro minority to view our national tardiness in historical perspective. Then, we might realize that the sheer helplessness of the black minority is due to a complacent self-satisfaction about our American democracy.

This complacence is neither new nor recent, for it has attended our national history. Thus, when our nation was born our Declaration of Independence not only gave us our ideals but seemed also to guarantee their realization. Then, the Civil War, retrospectively, gave us the assurance that we had guaranteed justice when the slaves were emancipated. Finally, with the industrial expansion after the last world war when so many problems on the social and economic level were solved, the Negro problem remained unsolved.

We must examine the illusions of these periods in turn. In the first period, that of the childhood of our nation, we assumed that we were a "peculiar nation." Abraham Lincoln in his famous Gettysburg address, expressed the ideal of our national purpose in terms of the Declaration of Independence. He said: ". . . our fathers brought forth on this continent a new nation, conceived in liberty and dedicated to the proposition that all men are created equal. Now we are engaged in a great civil war, testing whether this nation, or any nation, so conceived and so dedicated can long endure." It may be significant that Lincoln, though opposed to slavery, did not emphasize the contradiction between the ideal of equality and the frightful inequality between the slave owner and the slaves.

Our founding fathers when confronted with the constitutional task of creating a new nation out of the 13 independent colonies, some slave-holding and some not, did not spend too much time in debating the slave issue. They were more concerned with the evils of "monarchy" than those of slavery. They were not Machiavellian, but they were not above beguiling the slave states into the union by giving them a bonus representation in the federal congress equal to three-fifths the number of their voteless slaves. Thereby, they laid the foundation of the political power of the slave states. In its time that power threatened to impose slavery upon the territories or give them freedom to establish it. It was this which brought on the Southern secession defiance of the union, and not the Northern challenge to the slave institution. We may be grateful for the abolition movement, retrospectively, but it did not have the power to challenge slavery.

Lincoln, neither a racist nor an abolitionist, was quite honest when he wrote to Horace Greeley: "My primary purpose is to save the union." Lincoln may be described as a free soil, democratic nationalist. The Emancipation Proclamation was subordinate to the chief purpose of defeating the rebellion. According to the historian Richard Hofstadter, the Proclamation has "all the eloquence of a bill of lading." The plight of the Negro was not directly involved.

But the chief defect of an idealistic conception of emancipation was that the freed slaves were given no livelihood in land ownership nor opportunity to exercise a craft. The same government which passed the Homestead Act and settled white farmers on the frontier with free land gave no land to the poor ex-slaves. They were reduced to the status of debt-ridden sharecroppers on their former plantations. "By the 20th Century," the Report notes, "the Negro was at the bottom of American society."

Nor were Negroes admitted to the craft unions, a deprivation which became an even more grievous source of poverty in the industrial era which we will consider presently. After the ratification of the Fifteenth Amendment, which did endow them with a vote, Congress enacted several laws to guarantee the "equal protection of the law." But they were defrauded of this precious democratic political power which the white industrial workers used to such good advantage in curing modern industry of its early injustices. For they were defrauded of the right to vote by various devices, such as the poll tax, economic intimidation, and unconstitutional tests which required them to recite the provisions of the Constitution. In the South, the Negro was practically disenfranchised. In Louisiana, the number of Negroes registered in 1896 was 130,344. In 1900, after the State rewrote the suffrage provisions of its constitution, only 5,320 Negroes were able to be on the registration books. It was only in the Civil Rights Act of 1965 that provision was made for federal surveillance of voter registration, which eliminated the essential impotence of our Negro minority.

The climax of the contradiction in our national life which secured an affluent economy for the white man and increasing misery for the Negro minority occurred in our own period, in our industrial and technological era. In this era, we secured laborers for our burgeoning industry from all the poor of European origin and became famed as a "Melting Pot" of all nationalities; and . . . the industrial workers used their votes to force a reluctant middle-class culture to grant the workers the right "to organize and bargain collectively." Thus, an equilibrium of power in the industrial sphere increased the income of the workers. . . . But . . . modern industry had as one of its products the mechanization of cotton farming, and this robbed the Negro agricultural laborer of the only employment for which his minimal skills were adequate. Facing starvation in the former slave states, he drifted to our large northern cities and was kept alive by a welfare system, which the National Commission now examines and finds inadequate. Among its deficiencies, it must be recorded that all welfare systems give first priority to abandoned or deserted mothers and their children. It becomes necessary, therefore, for the father, if still part of the family, to pretend desertion and absent himself before the visit of the inquiring social worker. He is thus robbed of his dignity before his children; and his pretended desertion increases the number of fatherless families, which makes for a matriarchal structure of the ghetto family, thus contributing to the delinquency of young Negro males. The National Advisory Commission finds in the ghetto crime which erupted in the riots of 1967 a high incidence among young males from 16 to 25 years of age.

The high rate of unemployment among Negroes is due in great part to their lack of skill in a highly technical industry. But a study of modern construction unions and firms, undertaken by FORTUNE magazine, indicates that it may be due, in part, to color prejudice of either unions or firms. This may be inferred by the fact that if Negroes were hired in proportion to their percentage in the population, Negroes would have 37,000 more jobs as carpenters, 45,000 more as construction workers, 97,000 more as mechanics, and 82,000 more as metal craftsmen. All these crafts require apprenticeship but no technical education. One must assume, therefore, that color prejudice among white workers and in firms accounts as much for the high rate of Negro unemployment as does the defective education of Negro youths. This is a case where one cause of Negro poverty has persisted since post-Civil War days but also has become more and more grievous in our own period of industrial unionism.

The economic and political impotence of the Negro minority has thus shown that only the help of the whole national community can save the nation from the tragedy of a widening gap and contradiction between a free and affluent white nation and the increasing misery of its Negro minority. A tardy nation finally turned its attention to the task of redemption of that racial injustice. It is certainly significant that the "Negro revolution" of today dates from the Supreme Court decision of 1954 and the Civil Rights Acts of 1964 and 1965. This suggests that revolutions are generated, not by pure desperation, but by a combination of hope and frustration. The Negro revolution, significantly, began on the one hand in Martin Luther King's boycott of the Montgomery busses; and, on the other hand, with the official action of the nation's courts and government. . . . It has been one of the weaknesses in the revolution that its only economic weapon has been the boycott. The attempts to secure "open housing"—i.e., the abolition of ghetto segregation—by demonstrations has proved ineffective whether led by Dr. King in Cicero or Father Groppi in Milwaukee. It may be highly symbolic that the new Civil Rights Act, which included an open-housing provision, was secured only after the aura of martyrdom was attached to open housing by Dr. King's assassination in Memphis.

The revolution was thus a simultaneous birth of Negro discontent and of a new awareness in the nation of the flaws of injustice in a free society which had always prided itself on its democratic virtues. The Negro riots of 1966 and 1967 were not a part of that revolution; but they were an indication that the nation's new attitude had come too late to save the young unemployed Negroes who had no hope that new laws and court decisions could cure their hopeless frustration.

We have analyzed the moral situation in our nation which was created because we awakened too late in the modern period to the contrast between the tragic misery of our Negro minority and the pretensions of our national ideology, which had regarded our open society as capable of progressively solving all problems of racial justice through the moral idealism guaranteed at our birth by the Declaration of Independence, and allegedly also through the rebirth of our Civil War and emancipation. We have done this in order to give an adequate view of our contemporary "moral crisis," for it is the business of the church to remind the national community of its responsibilities, and remind it of its sins of omission and commission. . . .

The Negro community is served and integrated by the Negro churches. They must therefore be preserved, especially after the late Dr. Martin Luther King has shown how to cure the Negro church of pietistic irrelevance and to engage it in the struggle for justice. But there must be witnesses of transcendence over racial lines, by opening our churches to any Negroes who desire to worship with us, and by common clerical meetings and by integrated denominational and interdenominational meetings. Local church federations have conducted interracial young people's conferences for some time; and student organizations such as the YMCA and the YWCA have had interracial student conferences for some time. While these preceded the present Negro revolution, it may not be too radical to assume that such efforts were the original seed which sprouted in the present student cooperation between white and black students in the later effective "freedom rides" and "sit-ins" by which public places, restaurants, and public conveyances were integrated.

The churches are and ought to be interested in reforms of the present welfare systems. Many alternatives have been suggested. An annual wage for the Negro minority has the defect of lacking the assurance of dignity for Negro workers. The system of "negative income tax" had been suggested by a group of university economists. This would depend upon a legal establishment of a poverty minimum. Thereupon, individuals would be paid the value of exemptions for family and number of children which regular income taxpayers are allowed. The scheme would create direct responsibility of the federal government for averting dire poverty among the poor. It would not be more expensive than the increasingly dubious municipal welfare systems now are.

An even better support by the nation for an economically impotent Negro minority would be a system of scholarships for college students whose parents fall below the minimal poverty line and who show promise of intellectual leadership in the arts, in science, and in public life. These scholarships would be a solution to the problem of deprivation of our intellectual and technical resources which is revealed by the fact that parental poverty permits only 8% of our disadvantaged high school graduates to enter college. Naturally, there must also be provisions for helping Negro youth to acquire technical training for an increasingly technical culture. The anti-poverty program already has job training schools, some of which provide both training and minimal employment before the training is completed.

The report of the Commission is full of suggested programs to alleviate the injustices this complacent nation has enforced upon its Negro minority. The Commission's priorities deserve to be the order of business for the returning Congress and the newly elected government. The alternative to taking the Commission seriously is continued rioting. The rioting and ambushes of 1968 are even more ominous than those of 1967. The Commission has shown the way to correct the most grievous injustices, if the nation can muster the moral will realistically to meet the crisis.

All these old and new provisions could be negated because of expense. It is the high priority of an affluent society to lift the poor Negro minority from the vicious circle of technical ignorance, even illiteracy, sickness, and crime. It is certainly a higher priority than our military involvement in the civil war of an obscure nation. This futile war is costing us billions, while the problem of a helpless Negro minority, costing us half as much, has not been met. After almost two centuries of broken promises and pledges our debt to our Negro minority is immense and obvious, and its burden lies heavy upon our consciences.

The Moon Landing

[*The New York Times,* July 21, 1969, p. 7.] The lunar landing by American astronauts in July of 1969 occasioned a variety of opinions on the future of space exploration. Niebuhr was one of several prominent persons asked by the *Times* for his views on the question.

WITH all Americans I have a proper pride in the technical achievement of our first moon landing. It was a triumph of technology, teamwork, and discipline. Many speak of a "breakthrough" but one asks, breakthrough in what? The landing on the moon has been compared with the discovery of the new continent of America. But the moon is dead and barren of all natural and human life; and America was rich in all physical and historic possibilities.

But the chief reason for assessing the significance of the moon landing negatively, even while the paens of triumph are sung, is that this tremendous technical achievement represents a defective sense of human values and of priorities in our technical culture.

The same technology that gave us this triumph has created many of our problems. Our population at the beginning of the century was only twenty per cent urbanized; and now eighty per cent live in large cities. We have woefully neglected these urban centers. They are stinking with air and water pollution. Their inner cities are decaying. They are filled with Negro minorities, increasingly resentful, even in violent resentment, because they have been deficient in technical training and therefore subject to a much higher level of unemployment than the national average. The rich nation which can afford the technical "breakthrough" cannot offer the impoverished cities tax help to feed the hungry or educate the uneducated.

We are betraying our moral weakness in our very triumphs in technology and economics.

PART IV
BOOK REVIEWS

Emil Brunner, The Divine Imperative

["A Theology of Revelation," *New York Herald Tribune Books,* May 16, 1937, p. 20.]

By peculiar chance, the two most important theologians of Continental Protestantism are Swiss: Karl Barth, who is now teaching at Basle University after losing his position in Hitler's Germany, and Emil Brunner, who teaches at Zurich. Originally these two men were intimate collaborators and joint editors of a magazine which presented their viewpoint, usually known as "theology of crisis" or "dialectical theology." Their common emphasis was one in which the whole tradition of liberal Christianity was challenged as being merely a derivative of modern culture, with its humanistic, naturalistic and optimistic world view. Against it they proclaimed a theology of revelation which insisted that Christian faith must begin with the Biblical revelation as a basis and not seek to arrive at religious certainty by the ordinary processes of knowledge. They condemned both idealistic and empirical philosophy as equally futile and abortive. In recent years this partnership has been dissolved because Brunner tried to leave a place for "natural theology" in his system. He refused to set theology into diametric opposition to the general processes of thought and culture, but insisted that the philosophical questions about the meaning of existence are the starting point for Christian theology, even though he agreed with Barth that these questions can be solved only by faith and not by reason.

Since Brunner's less extreme interpretation of a theology of revelation is naturally more acceptable to the whole Anglo-Saxon theological and religious history, the simultaneous translation of three of his books will naturally be of interest to many theologians and philosophers.

The most important of the three volumes is a learned book on Christian ethics, entitled *The Divine Imperative.* The divine imperative is the love commandment, "Thou shalt love thy neighbor as thyself." This is an imperative, but it is not a law which can be codified. In opposition to this imperative he sets all the detailed moral and social codes by which society is ordered. The danger of religious legalism, a danger which is particularly apparent in orthodoxy, is that it imparts absolute religious sanctions to these relative moral codes. The danger of Christian liberalism is to believe that the love commandment is a simple possibility which any one may fulfill. Against the former Brunner insists that the love commandment is the only divine law. Moral codes are more or less relative to particular situations. They are important for the task of ordering life, but they stand under the criticism rather than the sanction of the love commandment. If a church declares, for instance, that God sanctions war because war may be a necessity of attaining justice, it is confusing two levels of morality. Conflict may be an inevitability in the attainment of justice, but the justice thus achieved is something less than love and must not be confused with it. On the other hand, the Christian liberal who declares that we must never fight because of the love commandment is equally wrong. He does not understand that we are living in a sinful world, in which life is set against life, and in which the immediate problem is the problem of justice.

In elaborating this thesis Brunner makes a detailed examination of all the various relative problems of social and political justice, and shows both the necessity and the inadequacy of political and coercive solutions. Since American Christian thought is informed by a rather simple moralism, it will not find Brunner's solutions acceptable. But a careful study of the book will at least persuade an honest reader to ask whether he has not stated the ethical problem too simply, and thus arrived too facilely at simple solutions. The book is the most important book in Christian ethics to appear since Troeltsch's *Social Teachings of the Christian Churches*.

In his *Philosophy of Religion* Brunner deals particularly with the epistemological problem and seeks to prove that the long and futile controversy between idealists and realists proves that the problem of knowledge cannot be solved by trying to interpret the external world in terms of ideas or ideas in terms of the external world. That the solution is possible only in terms of a faith in a creator God who is the ground and source of meaning in existence, a meaning in which the contrast between thought and extension is paradoxically dissolved.

In *God and Man* Brunner seeks to prove that a full appreciation of human personality as possessing a transcendent freedom over the processes of nature is possible only in terms of a faith which confronts that personality with an infinite God. All other alternatives reduce personality to nature and obscure the radical defect of sin in human action and life.

Every one of these books is a source of fruitful insight not only to theologians and religious people but to any unprejudiced thinker who has not raised modern naturalistic perspectives into a dogma which cannot be questioned. Brunner is a profound and searching thinker, fully versed in every historic philosophical problem. The danger in America is that liberal prejudices will prompt men to confuse Brunner's type of thought with obscurantist orthodoxy. It is to be distinguished from a wooden orthodoxy as sharply as from modern liberalism.

Benedetto Croce, History as the Story of Liberty

["Croce on History," *The Nation,* Vol. 152 (June 14, 1941), pp. 699–700.]

THE most obvious significance of Croce's book lies in the fact that this impassioned plea for liberty as the basic value of history has come out of Mussolini's Italy. Croce writes: "The adoration of the state or of might (*Macht*), born in Germany and introduced among other peoples, is nothing more than a base affection, not of citizens but of liveried servants and courtiers, for might as such, which is vainly adorned with sacred and moral emblems. . . . It is in fact stupid to exalt the state."

The ultimate significance of the book is that it represents a probably final word by a great philosopher on an aspect of philosophical thought which has been the preoccupation of his life—the philosophy of history. The fact that the book embodies a series of essays, not completely unified, detracts slightly, though only slightly, from its value as a comprehensive summary of his thought.

Croce approaches the problem of history from the standpoint of historiography. The question is: How can history be recorded? It cannot be recorded merely as a chronicle of facts and events, for these facts and events have a meaning. But their meaning can be appreciated only in the context of the meaning of the whole. Thus all but the most superficial historical records are involved in the problem of the meaning of history as such. Yet the historical perspective of the historian is itself relative, and his tendency is to interpret the whole past so as to justify a particular view of life, of society, and of history in his own present. (Thus a change in the party line prompts Communist historians to change their estimate of the character of Ivan the Terrible.)

Though Croce's entire work deals with this problem of historical relativism, he is inclined to underestimate its acuteness. Against all rationalists who imagine that it is easy to gain a position of rational transcendence over the relative stuff of history, he affirms the historical character of all thought; yet he criticizes Troeltsch for taking the problem of historical relativism too seriously. He believes that it is difficult, but not impossible, to achieve a "balanced judgment" which will correct the misinterpretations caused by the "arbitrary will of individuals." Yet the most plausible misinterpretations of the past arise not from an arbitrary or wilful falsification of historical data but from relative perspectives which are unconscious of the relativity and inadequacy of their position. The principle which underlies Croce's balanced judgment is that the interpretation of history must be governed by the total and perennial human situation and not by some particular human situation of this or that epoch. He finds the perennial factor he seeks in the struggle for freedom.

The most illuminating portions of Croce's work are his critical appraisals of alternative philosophies of history. He rejects naturalistic interpretations which regard history as scarcely more than an extension of the principle of evolution in biology. He is equally critical of eighteenth-century and later utopianism, which finds the meaning of history in the culmination of certain social values within history; and he wisely observes that to this utopianism it is not even clear whether history culminates in the realization of social ideals *ad finitum* or *ad infinitum*. Marxist utopianism is subjected to a particularly severe criticism because it seeks to realize perfect equality in history, a purpose which betrays it into the destruction of liberty. Croce points out, I think correctly, that equality is a transcendent principle of justice and not a simple possibility of history, and that where this is not understood, utopian dreams turn into tyrannical realities. Unfortunately his criticism of Marxism is marred by a failure to understand the economic, as against the political, factors in social life, an error which blinds him to the most illuminating elements in Marxist thought.

Croce's thought is, of course, closely related to Hegel's, but he is careful to underline the differences, as well as the similarities, between his and Hegel's philosophy: "Hegel aimed at resolving history into philosophy by giving it the movement of a system which develops and is completed in time. We, on the other hand, aim at resolving philosophy into history, considering it as an abstract moment of historical thought itself, and its systems as historical situations historically transient and historically justified." Thus the absurd culmination of history in the Prussian military state, or any similar realization of the eternal in the temporal, is avoided.

Croce is careful to point out that his idea of "balanced judgment" has nothing in common with either an impartiality which abstains from all judgments or a neutrality which merely finds a mean between contrasting judgments. The true historian "cannot remain immersed in events," but neither can he "stand outside them and move in a void. It is necessary to move through them, to feel the impact and the agony which they generate in order to stand above them, rising from suffering to judgment and knowledge."

But there can be no such transcendent judgment without a principle of judgment which transcends all particular historical circumstances. He finds this in the principle of liberty. "We always tend toward liberty and work for it even when we seem to be working for something else; liberty is realized in every thought and action that has the character of truth, poetry, and goodness." History is not the story of increasing liberty but the record of the fight for liberty under ever-changing circumstances. "The problem of freedom is perpetually resolved and perpetually recurs" because it is the desire for liberty which defines man as man.

One would think that the nature of man required community as well as liberty, and that history could be more adequately described as the interaction between these two partially contradictory and partially complementary desires. Croce tends to identify them. He declares: "These two requirements form a single need, for we cannot conceive of liberty without social organization, nor can we conceive of society and state without liberty, for it would no longer be human."

One difficulty with Croce's interpretation of history is that it seems to give no meaning to history as an ongoing process with cumulative effects. Croce admits that modern man must win his freedom against the tendency toward tyranny in a technical civilization, whereas primitive man asserted his freedom against the necessities of nature, but he seems to find no meaning in this historical development, tragic or otherwise.

Such criticisms and questions must not be allowed to obscure the greatness of this book. It is the work of a profound thinker who has meditated deeply on the most perplexing problems of human existence and who touches no issue without illuminating it.

Charles Norris Cochrane, Christianity and Classical Culture

[*The University of Toronto Quarterly,* Vol. 10 (July 1941), pp. 505–10.]

A REVIEWER of books is not frequently embarrassed by the fear that his appreciation may seem too extravagant; but that is the fear which assails me as I seek to express my opinion of a book which has given me more unalloyed pleasure than anything I have read in the past decade. This historical study of "thought and action from Augustus to Augustine" is a masterpiece. First of all it is truly a study of "thought and action" because the historian has mastered the thought of the classical world as thoroughly as he knows the movement of political and social events in the Roman Empire.

Even if the book were not a profound analysis and comparison of the classical and the Christian approach to life—that is, if the second half of the volume were entirely eliminated—it would still be a unique and distinguished study of the relation of the mind of classicism to the tragic events of a declining Rome, and a brilliant exposition of the thesis that what confronts us in the decline of Rome "is, in the last analysis, a moral and intellectual failure, a failure of the Graeco-Roman mind." I know of no history of this period of Roman culture which brings the thought of a Vergil, a Cicero, a Livy and a Plutarch into such relevance to the policies of statesmen and emperors as does this study. Nor is the thesis about the failure of the Roman mind stressed to the point of obscuring other factors in the decline of Rome. The analysis of the purposes and policies of the Augustan principate, for instance, reveals to what degree the empire overcame chaotic tendencies in republican-aristocratic Rome by policies which achieved a new unity and a higher justice but which had the seeds of ultimate decay within them. One recognizes the fatefulness of a policy which narrows the base of political authority in order to broaden the basis of political justice and imperial unity. It restores the health of the commonwealth at the expense of making its death more inevitable in the long run. Though Mr Cochrane does not point the moral or make explicit comparisons with our own day, one is struck by disturbing analogies with current political history, to the point of wondering whether he has not placed his finger upon a form of decay which operates without reference to the limitations of a classical culture and which may be repeating itself in the history of our own democratic civilization.

As for the basic thesis, that Roman decay was a revelation of the inability of the classical mind to come to grips with novel trends in history because its conception of *scientia* either reduced history to the uniformities of nature or raised it to the level of pure reason, I know of no historical treatise which has elaborated this criticism so brilliantly. As a matter of fact, modern culture has itself oscillated between Platonism and naturalism to such a degree, embracing either one or the other horn of the classical dilemma, that this historical study could have been written only by one who is no longer bound by the presuppositions of the traditional culture of our day. Professor Cochrane's criticisms of Cicero, for instance, are applicable with few reservations to most of the "liberals" of our epoch, though again he does not make this comparison, even if one may suspect him of having them in mind occasionally. Ciceronian classicism and modern liberalism make the common mistake of assuming that political life easily conforms to its ideal principles and that to state principles of justice is in effect to realize them.

Professor Cochrane's basic criticism of the classical mind is that its fundamental categories are unable to comprehend the realities of history. Whether it thinks in terms of mind or matter, of the causal chains of nature or of rational forms as the ultimate reality, it cannot deal with the uniqueness of the historical occasion or comprehend the freedom of human personality as it acts in history. History is, as a matter of fact, a curious compound of freedom and fate, which can be given meaning only in terms of some concept of providence which the classical mind cannot achieve. The Roman *fortuna* and the Greek *tyche* are, therefore, constantly subject to alternate interpretations which reduce the elements in history, beyond the control of the individual, either to an iron determinism or to pure caprice. In the one case the rationality of history is reduced to mechanism, which means that it is robbed of essential meaning. In the other case the irrational element in history overwhelms the concept of meaning. Stated in another way, there is no possibility of having a creative philosophy of history if meaningfulness is equated with rationality in either the idealistic or naturalistic sense.

Philosophers of history have analysed this problem before, but I know of no contemporary philosopher of history who has the command of detailed historical data to do what Professor Cochrane has done, which is to trace the practical influence of these defects in a philosophy upon the policies of statesmen and the history of an empire.

The vantage point from which the classical mind is criticized is that of Augustinian philosophy, though before Professor Cochrane arrives at Augustine he treats us to a remarkably astute historical analysis of pre-Augustinian Christian history, including the quasi-Platonism of Origen, the anti-rationalism of Tertullian (is Karl Barth the modern counterpart?), and the superficial and sentimental compound of politics and Christian morals in Constantine's clerical apologists.

Perhaps before going on to Professor Cochrane's discussion of Augustine it may be wise to say that I thought the book a most remarkable one before I had arrived at this treatment of Augustine. It was remarkable in distinction to all the analyses of Roman decline which have no real vantage point from which to view that decline because they are themselves based upon essentially classical presuppositions. But I hardly dared hope that Augustine would be understood so profoundly and that what is essential would be distinguished from what is peripheral in his thought with such fine discrimination. I had not dared to hope this because the religious world is only beginning to emerge from the arid wastes of a rationalized and sentimentalized Christianity, to appreciate Augustine. Why should a greater appreciation be expected in an historian and a philosopher?

Yet this is what we have in Professor Cochrane's book. It is a saner appreciation of the profundities of Augustine's great system of thought than most theologians could write because it has its eye upon what is essential and is not lost in theological minutiae. We see the importance of the doctrine of "original sin" as a basic category for the interpretation of history. We are helped to recognize the emphasis upon "grace" in Augustine's thought as a revelation of Christianity's understanding for the problem of power, vitality, and will in life as against the tendency to equate virtue with "form" or "order" or "ratio," in both classical and modern culture. Thus the confession of St. Paul, "to will is present with me but how to perform that which is good I find not," is again given the significance it deserves in interpreting human behaviour and the problems of human history. The whole discussion of Augustinian psychology, with its understanding of the essential unity of the rational and the volitional life of man, is profound.

Perhaps most remarkable of all is the understanding of the author for the relevance of Christian Trinitarianism to the interpretation of history. He writes, "In the Trinity, Christian wisdom discovers that for which Classicism had so long vainly sought, viz., the *logos* or explanation of Being and motion, in other words a metaphysic of ordered process." The reason this is so is that in the Trinitarian conception of God, the God who is revealed in history (Christ) and the God who transcends history (the Father) are recognized as equally God, though there is a slight emphasis, at least by implication, upon the priority of God the Father from whom the Son proceeds. Professor Cochrane sees, as no other historian to my knowledge understands, that the hair-splitting Christological controversies which preceded the Nicene definition of the Christian faith were something more than hair-splitting and really dealt with basic problems about the meaning of life and history. In the Christian definition of the ultimate, Professor Cochrane declares, Christianity "does justice to the element of truth contained alike in the claims of classical materialism and classical idealism." To understand history it is important not to regard "the body as the ultimate—i.e., the real principle of our existence as human beings"—nor yet to resolve the body, "as it was by the Platonists, into a mere 'appearance'. " This is to say, that a valid interpretation of history must take man's physical existence and his life in nature seriously on the one hand but must on the other hand realize that physical existence is not self-derived or self-explanatory or self-fulfilling. Professor Cochrane recognizes that the affirmations contained and implied in the Christian doctrine of Incarnation and Trinity, presuppose the Christian doctrine of Creation and that it is not possible to build a positive philosophy of history upon the Platonic concept of creation, according to which life comes into existence through the imposition of rational forms upon a previously given formless stuff thus "immobilizing reality and reducing it purely to terms of structure."

At one point I think I would concede more to the prejudices of the "modern mind" than Professor Cochrane seems to do. I would concede that Christian Trinitarianism is a non-Greek answer in Greek terms to the problem of the nature of Being. The Christian answer bridges the absolute gulf between the "passible" and the "impassible," between the Eternal and the natural in classical thought. It is precisely because Classical thought thinks only in terms of nature and the Eternal that it cannot understand history, which is something more than natural sequence. But to make the Christian affirmation in Greek terms involves the Christian faith in the nonsense of the distinctions about the two natures of Christ, etc.

These Christian affirmations can be made intelligible today if we concede that they are symbolic affirmations of ultimate *meaning*, but that they lack the kind of rational precision which the Nicene definition claimed for them. Christ is God, for Christian faith, not because it is possible to discern a "divine nature" curiously intermingled with a "human nature" in his person, but because in his life and death faith discerns the ultimate meaning of life, which is to say a revelation of the character of ultimate reality which transcends, and yet is involved in, the process of history.

I believe, as already suggested, that Professor Cochrane's book has a tremendous significance for the understanding of our own history, not only because there are obvious analogies between the decline of Rome and our own tragic period, but also because any profound analysis of the problem of history in any period is bound to throw light upon every period. Certainly our civilization can find no spiritual security or political peace within terms of the liberalism which has informed our democratic civilization and which failed so miserably to gauge the internal and external perils to which we have been exposed. We need a reorientation as urgently as did Roman classicism. In the broadest sense modern civilization requires an Augustinian reformulation of the problem of life and history. This reformulation cannot be the Catholic neo-Thomist version of Augustinianism because some of the dialectic of the Augustinian system is obscured in this version. Nor can it be the Reformation revival of Augustinianism because in this version the task of political justice is obscured. It will have to be more truly Augustinian than either traditional Catholicism or orthodox Protestantism; and it will certainly have to be more profound than either secular or Christian liberalism, which know literally nothing of the profound problems that engaged Augustine.

For these reasons the rediscovery of Augustine by one who is not a theological schoolman but first of all an historian and philosopher is of the greatest significance.

Søren Kierkegaard, Concluding Unscientific Postscript

["Kierkegaard's Message," *New York Herald Tribune Books,* November 30, 1941, p. 33.]

GRADUALLY the core of Kierkegaard's thought is being made available to American readers. With the publication of *Philosophical Fragments* two years ago and the *Postscript* now, it is possible for American students to gain a fuller conception of Kierkegaard's thought. The present translation of one of the most important works of the Danish philosopher and theologian was undertaken by the late Professor David Swenson, of Minnesota University, the greatest authority on Kierkegaard in America. His untimely death before completion of his task placed the translation of the remainder and the final editing upon Dr. Walter Lowrie, who has put all American students of philosophical and theological thought in his debt by the indefatigable zeal with which he has made Kierkegaard known to Americans. Dr. Lowrie will, incidentally, shortly bring out translations of two other major works of Kierkegaard, *The Sickness Unto Death* and *Fear and Trembling.*

No work of the Danish philosopher will give the reader a more comprehensive view of his thought world than this *Postscript.* In it we find Kierkegaard's polemic against speculative philosophy, and his indictment of philosophical systems, developed from every angle. Kierkegaard is the author of "existential" thinking. His impetus led to, or at least influenced, such divergent and yet related cultural developments as the dramas of Ibsen, the theology of Karl Barth and the "existential philosophy" of Jaspers and Heidegger.

Kierkegaard's quarrel with the philosophers is that they seek to give us a complete system of reality from an obviously finite prospective; but they delude themselves into believing that they have transcended their own finite position in their thought. They claim, in effect, to be God. "An existential system," declares Kierkegaard, "can not be formulated. Does this mean that no such system exists? By no means. Reality itself is a system—for God. But it can not be a system for any existing spirit. System and finality correspond to one another, but existence is precisely the opposite of finality. It may be seen from a purely abstract point of view that system and existence are incapable of being thought together; because in order to think existence at all, systematic thought must think itself abrogated, and hence as not existing. Existence separates and holds the various moments of existence discretely apart; systematic thought consists of the finality which brings them together."

Hegel's panlogism is the particular foil for Kierkegaard's polemic, but he makes it quite clear that his strictures are meant for all forms of rationalism and not limited to Hegelianism. In fact he varies between holding Hegel up to scorn and setting up the symbolic figure of a "Privatdozent." He is profoundly impressed by the relativity of all historic perspectives and the naiveté with which rationalistic professors are able to describe the "world-historical process" without recognizing that they are standing inside and not above this process. Thus the hybris of the historians leads to the most flagrant errors. The German historian, he declares for instance, has "place for only one Chinese thinker in the world process, but not a single German Privatdozent is excluded, especially no Prussian, since whoever has the cross makes the sign for himself first."

The philosophers forget that they are finite "existing" individuals, anxious for their life. "Because abstract thought is sub specia aeterni it ignores the concrete and temporal, the existential process, the predicament of the existing individual, arising from his being a synthesis of the eternal and the temporal, situated in existence." Fully to grasp the significance of Kierkegaard's thought it must be recognized that Hegelian rationalism produced the reaction of Marxist theory on the one hand and of Kierkegaard's on the other. Marx calls attention to the relativity of culture from the standpoint of the "ideologies" arising from the social situation. Kierkegaard's relativism is more individualistic, subjective and more "spiritual" in the sense that the "existing" individual is not defined as temporal merely by reason of being involved in the process of nature. The anxieties which make his reason something less than pure reason are not merely the anxieties of physical survival. They are the anxieties of a spirit which both transcends and is involved in the natural process.

The solution for the problem of the uniqueness, finiteness and insecurity of the individual and the relativity of his knowledge is not through a rational pride which obscures the "existential" character of all human knowledge but through a frank acceptance of the real situation: "My thesis is that subjectivity, inwardness is the truth." This inwardness is the truth in the sense that it discovers rather than obscures the real human situation: "Existing is ordinarily regarded as no very complex matter, much less an art, since we all exist. But really to exist, so as to interpenetrate one's existence with consciousness, at one and the same time eternal and as if far removed from existence, and yet also present in existence and in the process of becoming: that is truly difficult."

Here is the basis of "existential" philosophy in a nutshell. According to Kierkegaard speculative philosophy believes that the human problem is solved by emphasizing the transcendent character of mind over natural process until it is assumed that a final transcendence has been reached in some "universal" truth or system. The actual situation is that man remains a paradoxical creature who both transcends and is involved in temporal process, no matter how high his "spiritual" or cultural achievements may rise. Though the superficial observer may see similarities between Kierkegaard's doctrine of "inwardness" and mysticism, he is actually a foe of both mystic and rationalistic efforts to escape the temporal and reach some realm of eternal purity.

The inwardness of Kierkegaard expresses itself not in introversion to the point where contact with the external world is overcome. It expresses itself in "faith." And faith is the discovery of God as refuge against the perils of man's paradoxical existence: "Faith always gives thanks, is always in peril of life, in this collision of the finite and infinite which is precisely a mortal danger for him who is a composite of both." All those who think that religious faith is a substitute in the lives of simple people for what sophisticated people achieve by philosophy would learn a great deal from Kierkegaard's discussion of despair as the ultimate consequence of trying to comprehend the world from the standpoint of the finite self; and of faith as the possibility on the other side of despair.

Kirkegaard always skirts the abyss of the morbid and the eccentric in his profundities, and sometimes he fails to skirt it and becomes absurd. Thus the validity of his "inward" truth is vitiated by his insistence that it must have no relation to the general knowledge of the external world, or any philosophical attempt to understand the meaning of existence. If a truth seems to be "probable," according to Kierkegaard, it ceases to be a truth of faith. Faith is belief in the improbable. Thus faith is set in contradiction to human knowledge. This is the element in Kierkegaard's thought which gave rise to the theology of Karl Barth. It is an exposition of the dictum: Credo, ut absurdam est. It represents Protestant thought in its most radical form and in its tendency to be obscurantist in the realm of culture.

However profound Kierkegaard's insights into the ultimate mysteries of the individual soul and his understanding of the anxieties of existence which transcend all immediate fears of physical life, there is an element of perversity in his thought which makes a synthesis of faith and reason seem wise by comparison.

Jacob Burckhardt, Force and Freedom: Reflections on History

["The Historian as Prophet," *The Nation*, Vol. 156 (April 10, 1943), pp. 530–31.]

JACOB BURCKHARDT, the great Swiss historian, is known to the Anglo-Saxon world primarily as the author of *Civilization of the Renaissance*. But he was a philosopher of history as well as a historian, and thus it is fortunate that his reflections on history have finally been made available to us. The material represents Burckhardt's notes for three lecture series prepared for publication by his nephew. The translator, a young American historian, James Hastings Nichols, has added a very able introduction to Burckhardt's thought.

As a philosopher of history Burckhardt accepted neither the idea of progress which the French Enlightenment had popularized nor yet the cyclical interpretation of history which German romanticism had borrowed from classicism and which is best known to us in the thought of that late romantic, Oswald Spengler. On the whole he belonged in the tradition of Ranke, who sought to give history meaning not primarily as a continuum but in terms of the unique value of each moment and epoch. Burckhardt saw little more in the idea of progress than the vulgar illusion "that our time is the consummation of all time" and "that the whole past may be regarded as fulfilled in us."

In seeking to interpret the unique significance of various epochs he analyzed them from the standpoint of the particular balance achieved in each era among three factors—religion, culture, and the state. In making this analysis he refused to accept either the thesis that all cultural realities are but rationalizations of economic and political circumstances or the idealistic interpretation which makes cultural forces primary and all political and economic facts derivative. He had a lively sense of the constant interaction between civilization as the body of a culture and culture as the soul of a civilization, and his insights into these complexities represent a permanent antidote to simple deterministic theories, whether idealistic or materialistic.

Flourishing in the latter half of the nineteenth century and able to point up his historical reflections by contemporary observations which cover post-Napoleonic Europe until the Franco-German war, Burckhardt may be defined as a humanistic anti-democrat. He feared democracy because he thought it would contribute to the development of the totalitarian state. Some of his fears were prompted by the tragic history of France from the generous impulses of the Revolution to the sorry realities of the Napoleonic dictatorship. But it is not merely this bit of history that prompted his fears for the future but profound reflection on the necessity of a delicate balance between traditional cultural factors and emerging forces which he thought the rise of democracy had disturbed.

Though he had little understanding for the positive and creative elements in the bourgeois democratic movement and interpreted its passion for justice quite perversely, he must be credited with the most precise kind of prescience in regard to the twentieth century. No one predicted the modern totalitarian state more accurately. He was certain that its secularized power would be more vexatious than the sacred power of ancient states. He foresaw that peculiar relation between the industrial workshop and the battlefield, between industrial and military power, which characterizes modern militarism. He believed that modern tyrants would use methods which even the most terrible despots of the past would not have had the heart to use. "My mental picture of the *terribles simplificateurs* who will overrun Europe is not a pleasant one," he wrote a friend. Burckhardt even predicted fairly accurately to what degree a liberal culture in totalitarian countries would capitulate to tyranny through failure to understand the foe.

The accuracy of historical predictions does not necessarily validate the philosophical convictions upon which they are based. Burckhardt's thought, indeed, contains some apprehensions about democracy which history has refuted as definitely as it has justified his fears of the totalitarian state. Nevertheless, Burckhardt's view into the future was something more than successful guessing. He was one of the most profound historical minds of the last century, and he provides a quite unique illumination of our present difficulties.

Emile Caillet, The Clue to Pascal

[*Union Seminary Quarterly Review,* Vol. 5 (March 1944), p. 28.]

PASCAL'S significance in Christian thought is gaining new appreciation, and rightly so. World events have challenged the presuppositions and assurances of that interpretation of Christian faith which we know under the inclusive term of Pelagianism. They have given a new prestige to the Pauline-Augustinian strain in Christian history. Pascal was not only a Christian in the day of Descartes. He was an "evangelical" Christian who combined devotion to the Roman church with a form of piety derived from the Scripture in general and from the Augustinian interpretation of it in particular. This latter element in his thought makes him a heretic from the perspective of the Thomistic and neo-Thomistic reinterpretation of Augustine.

The author of this very moving and charming biography of Pascal is a Protestant layman, a professor of French literature at the University of Pennsylvania, who moved from Catholicism to Protestantism under the influence of Pascal, a fact which may prove to what degree Pascal's Catholicism is more evangelical than Roman. The biography assumes, rather than illumines, the significant emphases in Pascal's profound theological position. It can therefore not be regarded as an introduction to his thought. But if there are among those who have read Pascal's *Pensees* with only slight understanding of the spiritual conflicts in and out of which the thought of Pascal was fashioned, this book will paint in the background for us. Professor Caillet is particularly interested in the ascetic-saintly qualities of Pascal's life. His analysis of these personal qualities is very illuminating. For it proves to what degree a religious position which rejects the idea of the sinless saint in principle can nevertheless maintain an inner discipline which borders on the ascetic. Perhaps this peculiar rigor in Pascal might persuade us in the Protestant church, not to claim Pascal as our own too self-righteously. He was neither Protestant nor orthodox Catholic. Rather he exploited the "evangelical" content in Catholic spirituality to the full and a little beyond the limits of the rigid and fixed principles of Thomistic orthodoxy.

Gunnar Myrdal, An American Dilemma

[*Christianity and Society,* Vol. 9 (Summer 1944), p. 42.]

THIS long awaited study of Negro-white relations in America, undertaken by the Swedish social scientist under auspices of the Carnegie Corporation, fully justifies the expectations of those who hoped for a really comprehensive analysis of the most vexing problem in our democratic life.

The two volumes contain a thorough analysis of all of the various aspects of the racial issue in America. One of the most valuable contributions of the study lies in its refutation of all theories of racial antagonism which attribute it to one single factor, economic or political, historical or educational. Mr. Myrdal proves by his exhaustive examination of the data that every factor which contributes to racial friction is involved in every other factor. His total theory, therefore, amounts to an analysis of a vicious circle, which can be effectively cut at a dozen different points and must be attacked from every angle, educational and political, economic and religious.

This is the kind of study which every thoughtful student of our American life ought not only read but possess.

Friedrich Hayek, The Road to Serfdom

["The Collectivist Bogy," *The Nation,* Vol. 159 (October 21, 1944), pp. 478, 480.]

THE rise of totalitarianism has prompted the democratic world to view all collectivist answers to our social problem with increased apprehension. It is feared that any system of "planning" and any increase in the political control of the economic process will lead toward the omnipotent state. These apprehensions, expressed within reason, will be helpful in preserving democracy; for a too powerful state is dangerous to our liberties, even when its avowed purpose is the achievement of a more equal justice.

Friedrich Hayek, an Austrian economist now resident in Britain, raises these apprehensions to unmeasured proportions and scares himself back into an almost consistent laissez faire social philosophy, qualified only by the concession that the state may be permitted to guarantee minimal social securities. Some of our wise men have been heaping excessive praise upon this book, but I do not find it any more profound or prudent than Herbert Hoover's book on *Liberty* written about a decade ago.

No social philosophy dealing with only one of two contrasting perils which modern society faces is adequate to our situation. Dr. Hayek sees the perils of political power clearly enough; but there is nothing in his book to indicate the slightest awareness of the perils of inordinate economic power. He writes as if the automatic balances of a free competitive system were still intact, or would be, if the world had not been beguiled by collectivist thought. There is no understanding of the fact that a technical civilization has accentuated the centralization of power in economic society and that the tendency to monopoly has thrown the nice balance of economic forces—if it ever existed—into disbalance.

Hayek furthermore makes the mistake of assuming that if there is any political control of economic process at all it must be consistently dictatorial. "If," he declares, "the complex system of interrelated activities is to be consciously directed at all, it must be directed by a single staff of experts, and ultimate responsibility must rest with a commander-in-chief whose hands must not be fettered by democratic procedure." This is pretty close to pure nonsense; and all the experience of the democratic nations, deeply involved in planning production for war purposes, refutes it.

Denis de Rougemont, The Devil's Share

["Concerning the Devil," *The Nation,* Vol. 160 (February 17, 1945), pp. 188–89.]

THIS profound study of the reality and complexity of evil in human history was first published in French and is now presented in the English translation. Its thesis is an elaboration of the words of Baudelaire: "It is the devil's cleverest wile to convince us that he does not exist." In expounding this dictum De Rougemont is able not only to track down the general human trait of self-righteousness but to refute the tendency of modern culture to attribute evil in human life merely to ignorance, sickness, social maladjustment, or what not. De Rougemont believes that man has the capacity, because he has the freedom, to corrupt every virtue and to make any achievement the occasion for a new evil. The devil, he declares on scriptural authority, is legion. One way of obscuring the evil in us is to attribute it to natural necessity, when in fact it arises in the rational freedom of man. Another way is to find it embodied in a particular form in the enemy and therefore assume that it cannot be in us. Thus Hitler has contributed to illusions about evil in history because the depth of evil which he incarnated tempted us to believe that evil was inhuman.

"Hitler," declares De Rougemont, "was not outside humanity but within it. He was in us before he was against us. It is in ourselves that he rose up against us. And once he is dead he will occupy us without striking a blow if we do not admit that he is a part of us, the devil's part in our hearts." One need only consider the ubiquity of evils which arise from the impulse of domination and the various forms of racial and national pride which corrupt the democratic world to recognize the validity of this analysis.

De Rougemont does not, however, make the mistake of assuming that evil is equally embodied in all nations, classes, or individuals or that recognition of the internal and general character of potential evil makes it unnecessary to fight against the more flagrant forms of actualized evil. "If I resemble the criminal," he declares, "this does not justify the criminal but condemns me. . . . I will not let yonder criminal remain at large in order to give myself over to inner reforms." His doctrine is in short no quietistic escape from political and social tasks.

Many observers have called attention to the incipient forms of Nazism which are revealed in the democratic or civilized world in the impulse of imperialism and the pride of race, class, and nation. De Rougemont carries this analysis one step farther and proves that these social and political evils have their root in impulses of which no individual is wholly free.

Some modern readers will fail to profit by the author's profound analysis of the general sources of evil in human history and of the multifarious forms which it may take, because they will be affronted by the poetic and mythical symbols which he uses. But if they follow his logic they may find that these poetic symbols are practically essential tools of his analysis. If evil is thought of merely as cultural lag or natural inertia, these symbols are not necessary. But if we recognize historical evil as a corruption of human freedom, and not merely as some natural sloth which retards freedom, it will become apparent that the "devil" is a meaningful symbol. The devil is a fallen angel, a corruption of something good; and the corruption is caused by an excess rather than a defect of some particular vitality of life.

Carl Becker, Freedom and Responsibility in the American Way of Life

["A Living Process," *The Nation*, Vol. 161 (November 17, 1945), pp. 526–27.]

THE late Carl H. Becker was one of the truly wise men of our generation. He was historian, philosopher of history, and political philosopher, whose special interest it was to find a firmer foundation for democratic life and who had come to the significant conclusion that eighteenth-century thought was an inadequate basis for the continued growth of democratic thought and the constant readjustment of the democratic process.

In a posthumously published series of lectures titled *Freedom and Responsibility in the American Way of Life* he sums up his conclusions so perfectly that they well might have been the intended summation of his life work. "The nature of freedom and responsibility is such that they cannot be discussed," he declares, "still less dealt with to any good purpose, separately." The eighteenth century had equated democracy with the assertion of inalienable rights. Becker shows that the rights and liberties must be exercised with a higher sense of responsibility for the common good; otherwise the community is forced to abrogate them in the interest of justice. "The owners of English cotton mills in the 1830's," he writes, "enjoyed freedom of contract as a cherished liberty; but for the anemic women and children who contracted to work in the mills because the alternative was starvation, it was a species of wage slavery."

While Becker emphasizes the importance of character in the operation of democracy ("the preservation of our freedom depends less upon the precise nature of our Constitution and laws than upon the character of the people"), he does not belong to the moralists who would solve political issues by moral means only. He is constantly looking for the best possible instruments for the preservation of both justice and liberty. He is certain that the eighteenth century was wrong in assuming that an unmanaged economy would make for justice, and he nicely debunks the privileged classes of today who use that creed for their own ends. He understands that collectivism finally destroys freedom, but is also certain that there must be increasing control of the economic process in the interest of justice.

He is critical of all uncritical devotion to written constitutions and to cherished forms of the past because he understands that democratic life is a living process which requires constant readjustments to new situations. Becker is in short the kind of guide whose loss one regrets the more deeply in a day in which interested dogmatists speak unctuously of the "American way of life," while they seek to preserve some special privilege or evade some obvious responsibility of their power.

John C. Bennett, Christian Ethics and Social Policy

[*Christianity and Society,* Vol. 12 (Winter 1946–47), p. 41.]

NO book has appeared in recent years which comes closer to expressing the most fundamental convictions of the Fellowship which sponsors this journal than this volume by one of our members, Professor Bennett. It is a book which illumines the absolute character of the moral obligation in Christian faith in its relation to the endless complexities of actual social situations in which the oligation to one's neighbor must be applied.

Professor Bennett discusses the four basic Christian strategies in this field: (a) The Catholic strategy which approaches all specific issues upon the basis of fully defined mediate as well as ultimate ethical norms. (b) The strategy of withdrawal from the more ambiguous social responsibilities for the sake of individual perfection. This is best exemplified in modern pacifism. (c) The identification of Christianity with particular social programs, of which most Christian socialist movements of the past were exemplars. In dealing with this strategy Professor Bennett calls attention to our Fellowship as holding such a position with reservation. (d) The strategy of the double standard for personal and public life, of which traditional Lutheranism is the best example.

Dr. Bennett does not find any of these strategies adequate and therefore suggests a fifth, which contains some of the elements of the previous four. It is "one which emphasizes the relevance together with the transcendence of the Christian ethic and which takes account of the universality and persistence of sin and the elements of technical autonomy in social politics."

The elaboration of this fifth strategy and his discussion of the role of the church includes a definition of what Dr. Oldham and Dr. Bennett have defined as "middle axioms." These are working principles of justice which are somewhat in the category of the Catholic "relative natural law" but they do not have the fixed character of the latter. They are pragmatically conceived and are fluid, requiring periodic adjustment to the moving historical situation. Dr. Bennett's definition of these middle axioms brings out the full wisdom of his social theory and his ability to do equal justice to the ultimate principles of right by which conduct must be guided and the endless varieties of situations to which it must be adjusted.

His final note on "natural law" comes to what seems to me the correct conclusion that "it is a mistake to believe in existence of a self-sufficient reason that always knows the good but it is equally a mistake to deny that Christian moral conviction overlaps with a broader knowledge of the moral order that confronts Christians and non-Christians alike." This is a position which is neither Catholic nor radical-Protestant. It underlies the whole of Professor Bennett's theory of social policy and is, I am convinced, a truly ecumenical position in Christian social theory. It does not merely split the difference between opposing Christian strategies. It has the possibility of becoming a new creative center for such strategies.

Hans J. Morgenthau, Scientific Man versus Power Politics

[*Christianity and Society,* Vol. 12 (Spring 1947), pp. 33–34.]

THIS very important little book has been, so far as I know, completely ignored by the journals of opinion, probably because the prejudices and idolatries of a scientific age, which it attacks, are still dominant in most of our intellectual centers. Professor Morgenthau gives an authoritative, and it seems to me a final, refutation of the school of thought which assumed that all the vexing problems of man's social existence could be solved if only we could extend the "methods of science" from the field of nature to the realm of history and society, or that all our difficulties in creating a world community can be attributed to the cultural lag.

After surveying the literature of this type of rationalism in the past two centuries, Dr. Morgenthau dissects its errors, which may well be reduced to two primary ones. The one error is to imagine that events in history follow as necessarily from previous causes as do occurrences in nature. Human freedom introduces endless contingencies in the realm of history which make all predictions of the future precarious. He is convinced, therefore, that the idea of social planning, upon the basis of scientifically established estimates of all social factors, contains hazards which are not envisaged in the thought of even such moderate advocates of social planning as Karl Mannheim. "The purer the intention and the more comprehensive the plan," he declares, "the wider will be the gap between expected and actual results." On the other hand he does not regard historical reality as a realm of pure contingency. For this reason there is a real place for social sciences. "The contingent character of social reality," he writes, "is only one of its aspects. . . . Its contingencies are not mere chaos but follow each other with certain regularity and are subject to a certain order. What to the contemporary observer appears mere chance—appears in retrospect as a meaningful process."

The second reason why a purely scientific attitude toward social reality is not possible is because the scientist is never a disinterested observer, as in the field of the natural sciences, but always explicitly or implicitly an interested participant. He is subject to various pressures; and whatever disinterestedness he may achieve is therefore a moral and religious, rather than a purely scientific achievement: "The greatness of a scholar does not alone depend upon his ability to distinguish between true and false. His greatness reveals itself above all in his ability to select from among all truths those which ought to be known."

The consequence of the element of contingency in the realm of history and of the relativity in the observers of history makes it impossible to reduce the stuff of history to pure rationality. For this reason history will remain a realm of contending social forces, and these forces will embody power and use power. Dr. Morgenthau shows very clearly why it is vain to hope for the gradual elimination of the moral ambiguity of politics through historic development. He contends that every moral action is more ambiguous than the abstract analysis of a moral action and that a political action is doubly ambiguous, for it involves the power impulses of a group. The general thesis is one which is not unfamiliar to readers of this journal. The book should have a wider acclaim than it will probably get.

Perry Miller, Jonathan Edwards

["Backwoods Genius," *The Nation*, Vol. 169 (December 31, 1949), p. 648.]

PERRY MILLER'S biography of Jonathan Edwards is one volume in the series of "American Men of Letters." Whether America's first and foremost theologian belongs in that category may be a matter of dispute. But undoubtedly it was very important for the understanding of our culture that someone should give a fuller appreciation of the significance of this backwoods genius than is found in previous biographies. For these, however excellent, have never reached an audience beyond a limited number of theological-minded readers. In the history of American culture Edwards is a nebulous figure condemned as a fire-and-brimstone revivalist who sought vainly to preserve pessimistic "Old World" religion in the roseate ethos of this new and "free" world or else praised as a profound philosophical mind, without elucidation about the significance of the fruits of his mind.

The task of interpretation was obviously reserved for Perry Miller—who has burrowed into the mind of our New England ancestors more successfully than any other American historian—partly because he brings to the task the gifts of an imaginative artist and partly because he approaches his subject with a sympathy which a twentieth-century mind cannot easily give to an eighteenth-century Calvinist but without which no subject of history can yield its secret to even the most diligent inquirer. The depth from which Miller restores Edwards is accurately described by him as follows:

> Artists who shared the historic Christian insight into what hitherto was called sin had a hard time in America. Hawthorne won an audience for his romances but none for his theology. Melville's cry that an inscrutable malice sinews the White Whale was not heeded. Mark Twain's recognitions were concealed by indirections. Edwards, it is true, had followers in the dynasty of New England theologians, but they petrified his theology, reduced his revivalism to a technique for mass manipulation, and then destroyed the architecture of his thought. . . . By this process Edwards was lost to the American tradition. . . . Even in the twentieth century, when the smiling aspects largely ceased to smile and Hawthorne, Melville, and Mark Twain were reevaluated, Edwards remained identified with what Dr. Holmes called "the nebulous realm of Asiatic legend."

Miller's restoration is a brilliant biographical study. It is not easy to say in a brief review why this study makes so profound an impression upon the reader. It is partly due to a very sophisticated analysis of Edwards's thought, in which the biographer reveals how the new wine of the thought of Locke and Newton in the old wineskin of New England Calvinism produced a quite remarkable system of thought. As the author traces the strands of eighteenth-century empiricism and rationalism in the thought of Edwards, one feels that one is reading a detective story. But the profound impression made by the book also derives from the artful way in which the exploration of a mind is related to the social history of New England and to the tragic drama of Edwards's personal life. One sees how, in a theological age, social forces are theologically expressed and why Edwards enraged the developing plutocracy of New England. They had managed to insinuate a growing Yankee complacency into their traditional faith, and Edwards challenged their self-deceptions. This also led to his personal undoing, for the parish of Northampton, which once prided itself upon being the center of the great awakening, tired of the rigor of his preachments and banished him. The tragedy was not "pure" because even Edwards's rejuvenated Calvinism was not free of the moral arrogance which corrupts all systems of religious legalism.

Northampton banished Edwards as the Athenians banished Aristides the Just. A moral censor who is not conscious of sharing our frailties finally becomes intolerable.

It is foolish to challenge an author in such complete command of his material. But I must confess to a suspicion that Miller sometimes makes Edwards more modern or more relevant to modernity than he is. I am not sure that the only way to overcome "Arminian" moralism is to espouse as strict a determinism as that of Edwards. In a brilliant chapter on The Objective Good, Miller traces the relation of Edwards's thought to that of Newton's, showing that Newton was afraid to delve too deeply into the mystery of the coherence of the world, which had been atomized by his exploration of efficient cause. Edwards resorted to the Christian doctrine of creation and asserted that "it must needs be an infinite power which keeps the atoms together—which resists all finite power, how big soever, as we have proved these bodies to be." Miller thinks this does not mean, for Edwards, that "God acts *ab externo* to press the million pieces of stone into the form of a rock." Yet there must be something of the old Calvinist conception of "special providence" in the remark that "nothing but Deity, acting in that particular manner in those parts where he thinks fit," holds the world together. In so far as this conception is not strictly Calvinist, it must have borrowed something from the Neo-Platonic-Augustinian notion that divine power prevents being from degenerating into non-being. One might raise similar questions about Edwards's alleged "naturalism" when he is expounding a fairly traditional doctrine of the realm of "grace" above the level of the natural good. But why cavil? What is important is that reluctant twentieth-century readers should read a book to which they might not be naturally drawn. If they will not read it in order to explore Edwards's mind they might read it to explore Miller's. They would be greatly profited on that basis; and they would learn into the bargain something about a seminal period in our spiritual history.

Arthur Koestler and others, **The God That Failed,** *edited by Richard Crossman*

["To Moscow—and Back," *The Nation,* Vol. 170 (January 28, 1950), pp. 88–90.]

THIS symposium of confessions of ex-Communists and ex-fellow-travelers, recording their enchantment and disenchantment with communism, can be defined, without stretching a point, as a work of art. It has the artistic merits of a good mosaic in which the separate parts are obvious but do not destroy the consistency of the pattern. But more than that it has the artistic virtue of illustrating a universal spiritual tragedy in Western history by means of the highly particular autobiographical notes of six sensitive men of letters. Of the six, one is Italian, one English, one French, one German-Hungarian, and two are American, one white and one Negro. Their experiences varied. They had this in common: they were drawn to communism by their abhorrence of injustice in capitalist society, and they were finally repelled by the greater injustices of the Communist tyranny.

The moving power of their several chronicles derives not merely from the unity of the theme embodied in significant variations but also from the reader's sense that they are recording a tragedy in which all of us have been involved. That tragedy is that the moral protest against the injustices of our civilization should have been organized in a movement which replaced the whips of injustice with the scorpions of tyranny. Most of the six confess to having entertained the error of assuming that a historical force which challenges an unjust system thereby proves its own justice. Some required only a short time and some took longer to reconcile themselves to one of the most tragic aspects of human history—namely, the possibility that an evil may be supplanted by a more grievous one.

The chronicle of their several pilgrimages toward the Communist Utopia contains, as the editor, Richard Crossman, suggests, the single theme of a passion for justice, inspired by more or less unconventional Christian convictions, which Silone movingly relates to the Franciscan tradition of his native Abruzzi. Only two experienced the injustices of our world in their personal fate—the two proletarians, Silone and Wright. Silone tells a tragic tale of feudal injustice in his native village, which opened his eyes much as Marx's eyes were opened by the severity which was the lot of peasants who picked up fallen wood in the forest preserves of Westphalia. Richard Wright saw the Communist movement as a bond of universal fellowship in which a Negro American might find meaning. The common faith which drew all of them is nicely expressed by Gide:

> My conversion is like a faith. My whole being is bent toward a single goal, all my thoughts, even involuntary, lead me back to it. In the deplorable state of distress of the modern world the plan of the Soviet Union seems to point to this. . . . If my life were necessary to assure the success of the Soviet Union I would gladly give it immediately.

This strong "will to believe" in an earthly paradise, which frequently persists for months and years after evidence accumulates that the paradise is a hell of tyranny and chicane, is also a universal characteristic of the confessions. Wright and Spender are most quickly disillusioned. In three cases experiences in Spain, and the conviction that Russia was on the right side in that struggle, postponed the final dénouement.

How did the disillusionment take place? Whether, as in the case of Silone, Communist tyranny was experienced in direct contact with the highest Russian oligarchs, or, as in the case of Wright, the arbitrariness and inhumanity of authoritarianism became known through contact with the petty Communist bosses of Chicago, the experiences and reactions are similar. Koestler and Gide are both outraged by the extravagant privileges enjoyed by intellectuals in Russia so long as they wear the yoke of tyranny meekly. Gide is primarily concerned with the corruption of culture and art under a dictatorship. Fischer began to doubt as he observed the various purges. He throttled his doubts until the Nazi-Soviet pact finally destroyed the structure of his faith.

Koestler is most revealing and most amusing in recording the elaborate system of self-deception by which an essentially honest man tries to preserve both his loyalty and his self-respect amid the wild confusion of changes in the party line. Wright adds a nice bit of wry humor to this analysis by reporting an incident in which a lunatic, escaped from an insane asylum, could threaten the standing of a loyal member of the John Reed Club because the club was under the erroneous impression that the lunatic was armed with party authority. "What struck me most about Russian Communists, even in such exceptional personalities as Lenin and Trotsky," reports Silone, "was their utter incapacity to be fair in discussing opinions which conflicted with their own." Most of the confessions reveal not only the inhumanity which is derived from uncontrolled and uncriticized power but the cruelty which is the fruit of a fanatic and absolute creed.

It was the need not for freedom as such but for the preservation of the dignity of man which finally convinced these men that their god had failed. For Koestler this sense of an outraged human dignity in the Soviet system came as a kind of religious illumination in a Spanish prison. He learned "that man is a reality and that mankind is an abstraction, that men cannot be treated as operations of political arithmetic, . . . that ethics is not a function of social utility and charity not a petty-bourgeois prejudice but the gravitational force which keeps civilization in its orbit." "There is no freedom in a dictatorship," declares Fischer, "because there are no inalienable rights. The dictator has so much power and the individual so little that the dictator can take away any right which he gives." Spender finds the dignity and value of the individual destroyed by faith in the inexorable forces of history, by a determinism which leaves no scope for individual conscience. "In one's absorption with an ideal," writes Fischer, "it is possible to imagine that one generation may be sacrificed for its descendants. But sacrificing people may become a habit into the third and fourth generation."

The editor having been discerning, only essentially healthy ex-Communists are included in this group of penitents. Those who have been maimed, who have turned to reaction or to another form of totalitarianism or have become cynical are rightly not heard from. The six remain devoted to the cause of social justice, but they have found that freedom is a more important component of justice than they had realized in their pilgrimage to Moscow.

I find only one lack in this moving series of confessions. None of the authors speculate very profoundly on the reasons which persuade modern men to seek a Utopia or why their dreams turn into nightmares. If a political scheme of redemption endows the oligarchs of its system of power with the halo of absolute sanctity, they exercise their power more vexatiously than the traditional lords of history, who were unable to claim so much sanctity. Was not the pilgrimage of the several authors of the symposium to the Utopia of Moscow a symptom of the false yearning in our whole culture for absolute goals in history, whereas we must be content with fragmentary and tentative achievements of the good in all our historical striving? Does not the charity that Koestler calls the "gravitational force which keeps history in its orbit" derive from a humility that recognizes the incomplete and fragmentary character of every scheme of justice, so that the highest form of perfection in history is incompatible with any claim that we have the final form of perfection in our keeping?

Karl Barth, Dogmatics in Outline

["Swiss Theologian," *New York Herald Tribune Books,* September 10, 1950, p. 43.]

FOR Americans, even in the religious world, Karl Barth, Swiss scholar and neo-orthodox Protestant theologian, is still a nebulous figure about whom they have heard vague reports. This book, an exposition of the Apostles' Creed, will give such readers a good general view of Barth's system of thought. In twenty-three chapters, originally delivered in 1946 as lectures at Germany's University of Bonn, Mr. Barth discusses the basic tenets of Christianity.

The main emphasis, as always in Barth, is upon the Bible. In his view the character and purpose of God could not have been anticipated and cannot be understood by any of the disciplines of culture or philosophy. The Biblical revelation is essential; faith, not reason, is the basis of Christian knowledge.

Metaphysical and religious speculation, Mr. Barth holds, merely results in fashioning God in some human image. If, for instance, the Scripture speaks of God as "Father," Mr. Barth assures us, this term has nothing to do with any experience of human fatherhood. On the contrary, "true and proper Fatherhood resides in God and from this Fatherhood of God what we know as fatherhood among men has been derived."

The rigorous rejection of every commerce between theology and the disciplines of culture drives Mr. Barth further and further into literalism. And this, in turn, involves him in some rather strange social and moral judgments, as, for example, in his discussion of anti-Semitism. At the same time, being an imaginative and poetic person, he is capable of indulging in fanciful speculation on such a subject as the Virgin Birth. In every case his exposition is presented with a certain dogmatism and *ex cathedra* authority.

Dogmatics in Outline is not only a relatively simple introduction to Barthian theology, but it reveals quite clearly why Mr. Barth has been so effective an antidote to sentimental versions of the Christian faith—and also why the antidote has not been very effective in the Anglo-Saxon world.

Louis Fischer, The Life of Mohatma Gandhi

["Gandhi and Non-Resistance," *The New Leader,* Vol. 33 (September 16, 1950), pp. 20–21.]

WHEN a Hindu fanatic assassinated Mahatma Gandhi in January 1948, the crown of martyrdom was added to the aura of sainthood with which his contemporaries had already invested this curious little man. He had elicited religious veneration in his own nation and something very like it in the Western world. Many lives have been, and will be, written to record, appreciate and interpret this remarkable personality. Among these, it is safe to predict, Louis Fischer's will take an honorable place. It was almost foreordained that Louis Fischer should perform this task. Fischer's radical social and political convictions, his disillusionment with Communism and his consequent search for a more viable "revolutionary" creed would naturally direct his interest toward Gandhi. Furthermore, his benignity of spirit establishes a bond of sympathy with Gandhi's unique approach to life, while his journalistic objectivity prevents the book from being merely the adulation of a disciple.

The biography is first of all a diligent analysis of the record. We can follow the history of the man from his childhood, through his first political efforts in behalf of the Indian minority in South Africa, through the various campaigns for Indian independence, to the final climax of victory and defeat. For victory and defeat were curiously mingled in his final days. The independence of India crowned his labors with success, while the partition of India and the frightful internecine strife between Moslems and Hindus revealed how little his doctrine of non-violence had really mastered the spirit of the people. He regarded the partition and the attendant violence as his nation's disavowal of his doctrine and alternated between a sense of defeat and frantic efforts in his final days to heal the breach between Moslems and Hindus. The chapters in which these efforts, including his last fast, are recorded belong to the most poignant in the book.

The special value of Fischer's biography lies in the combination of diligent research into the record with personal reactions. Fischer spent many hours with Gandhi and some of his interviews are given verbatim. Unlike another recent book on Gandhi, which tells us more about the author's sentimental, not to say hysterical, reactions than about Gandhi, Fischer's questions and comments are adroitly calculated to elicit characteristic responses from his subject for the purpose of interpreting him to the Western world. Fischer had obviously established a relation of bantering friendship with Gandhi which serves to reveal Gandhi's sense of humor as well as his characteristic credos.

Despite the great achievements of this biography, it does leave some questions unanswered. Gandhi has been frequently described as a saint in politics. He did combine a remarkable degree of political shrewdness with religious absolutism. Did he thereby establish a moral norm for politics which could be emulated generally? Is it possible in the Western world to use the prestige of saintliness as an "instrument of policy" as Gandhi did when he fasted in order to achieve political objectives? Could that be done anywhere else but in India, where special religious presuppositions create a climate for that kind of politics? Heroic martyrdom is not unknown in the Western world; but the threat of martyrdom as a political weapon would hardly avail among us. It might not even be regarded as decent.

More important is the question about Gandhi's pacifism. This pacifist creed assumes that non-violence as a method is a guarantee that love is the motive of an action. Fischer does not fully analyze Gandhi's peculiar logic in regard to non-violence. He accepts Gandhi's own estimate of the similarity between Tolstoy's doctrine of non-resistance and his own doctrine of non-violent resistance. His chapter on the relation between Gandhi and Tolstoy is historically informative; but it does not probe into the difference between the two doctrines. A doctrine of pure non-resistance may have ultimate religious significance above the claims and counter-claims of political life. But it can have no real political significance; for politics must deal with the competition of interests and claims. If politics is not to be completely amoral, the question of the justice of the claims must be raised. But if political idealism is not to be completely irrelevant, the question of how one's own claim is to be effectively made must be raised.

A doctrine of non-resistance implies a politically irrelevant saintliness which would rather be defrauded than make any claims. A doctrine of non-violent resistance provides for the making of claims. Thus Gandhi seeks to achieve Indian independence by resisting British imperialism. Gandhi assumes that the method of non-violence guarantees the moral acceptability of the end for which non-violence is used. In fact, he equates the motive of love so completely with the particular method that he can even claim that violence (as in the case of his support of the first World War and the burning of English cloth) may be mysteriously compatible with the spirit of non-violence. What he probably meant was that the ends which he sought in these instances were morally above reproach, i.e., in conformity with the principle of love which he advocated.

The principle of non-violent resistance thus stands midway between a politically irrelevant ideal of non-resistance and a political ethic which will use violence if the end seems morally justified (as, for instance, our present resistance to aggression in Korea). Is this position a tenable one, and can it become the basis of a political ethic which will ultimately overcome the tragic conflicts in human history? Fischer frequently suggests that Gandhi, as all great spirits of history, has laid the foundation for something which must be judged, not by the short span of his own life-time but by a longer span of history. It is more probable that Gandhi, as unique spirit, will live beyond his age; but that his peculiar doctrine of non-violent resistance will have no more and no less validity two hundred years from now than in the present. It has validity insofar as it is always important to make human conflicts of interest non-violent if possible. It has no validity insofar as it is offered either as a certain way of achieving a morally acceptable goal or as an escape from the moral ambiguities of political life.

On this point, Gandhi's own final days are instructive. He consistently refused to accept the partition of India, even after his government had acquiesced in it. His political alternative was that it would be better for India to fall into chaos than to accept partition. But chaos is never a possible alternative for a responsible statesman. Gandhi's willingness to entertain the alternative rested upon his belief that human nature was as good as the water in the ocean is pure, even though some parts of the ocean may at times be muddy. He was confident, in other words, that Hindu-Moslem animosities were only a passing phase in the relation between these two communities. Such a faith is not politically relevant when statesmen must decide whether antipathies between two portions of a community are so deep that separation would lead to less conflict than an enforced unity.

We can, in short, have a full appreciation of Gandhi as a great religious and political leader without assuming that his creed can become normative either for India or for the rest of the world. In any event, we must weigh the normative quality of the creed carefully. This has not been accomplished in Mr. Fischer's otherwise most valuable biography.

Paul Tillich, Biblical Religion and the Search for Ultimate Reality

[*Union Seminary Quarterly Review,* Vol. 11 (January 1956), pp. 59–60.]

PAUL TILLICH'S influence on American theology has been a very profound and creative one, ever since Hitler unwittingly enriched our whole culture, and our theology in particular, by forcing him to emigrate to our shores. He has labored for two decades in the American theological vineyard and his influence has been a constantly growing one. His unique contribution was partly derived from his very great gifts of both mind and heart and partly from his complete mastery of both the philosophical and theological disciplines. He has lived constantly on many boundaries, but most of all on the boundary of theology and philosophy.

This little volume, embodying lectures given at the University of Virginia, is priceless because it is an even clearer statement of his position than many of his larger volumes. It has the additional merit that it states the contrast between an "ontological approach" to reality and the "radical personalism" of Biblical religion with more precision than many of his critics have stated it. Of course he also affirms the common concern of Biblical religion and the metaphysical quest. This common concern is his preoccupation and he allows himself one of his rare personal outbursts in theological debate when he declares that the cavalier and condescending attitude of some theologians toward philosophy "infuriates" him. He criticises Harnack and Ritschl for interpreting the theology of the early Greek fathers as a capitulation to Greek ways of thought. It was, Tillich declares, a necessary enterprise because it related the Biblical concern for the ultimacy of the divine, in contrast to all idolatrous faiths, with the metaphysical search for ultimate reality. If God is not being itself or the "power of being," he is only one being among other beings and therefore not the true God.

The merit of Tillich's thought is that he not only states the issue between Biblical faith and the metaphysical search for "ultimate reality" fairly but that he tries to do justice to the peculiar insights of Biblical religion. He does not, like Hegel, regard Biblical faith as merely a crude form of picture thinking, which philosophy must refine. He insists that it is important for the religious person to experience the "holy" or the being which is of "ultimate concern" for us as a person, because he can not "be less than we are" which presumably means that he must have the same freedom which we have as persons. Prof. Hartshorne would say that he must have the capacity for self-transcendence, a capacity which is very difficult to bring within an ontological system. Incidentally, we face a semantic problem at this point: for if we define as "ontological" everything which concerns "being" there need not be any conflict between Biblical-poetic and philosophical ways of apprehending the divine. But if "ontology" means the "science of being" it may be questioned whether the mystery and meaning of the divine can be comprehended "scientifically" or rationally and philosophically. Tillich admits this when he declares that the theologians were right in speaking of creation "ex nihilo," thereby defining creation as a mystery beyond the bounds of rational thought. If it is brought within the bounds of reason God is always transmuted into either the "structure" of being or into the "ground" of being from which particular beings emanate.

Tillich is certainly right in calling attention to the necessity of using philosophical tools in eliminating all forms of idolatry (that is, the ascription of ultimacy to finite values and powers as the center and source of meaning) but he probably does not take seriously enough that the prophets of the Old Testament were as rigorous as the Greek philosophers in their rejection of all finite Gods. They did this by their insistence that the true God was the creator of the world.

The real problem with Tillich's very imposing system of thought is, for one admiring colleague at least, that he interprets the religious problem correctly as the problem of the "meaning of our existence" but somewhat dubiously equates the question of meaning with the question of being and non-being. He would overcome despair by proving to men that their contingent being is grounded in ultimate being. This may be an answer for the metaphysically inclined and gifted. But it is more probable that the real question about meaning is not whether the world rationally coheres in some structure of being but whether the coherence can give meaning to the strange drama of human existence, considered either individually or collectively. This drama has tangents of meaning and suggestions of meaninglessness. The threats of meaninglessness are not overcome by a faith which asserts the ultimate coherence of things, but by a faith which takes the incoherences into its system of meaning. That is why the love and trust of our fellows as indices of the character of ultimate reality may more frequently save us from despair than metaphysical speculations about being and non-being. This is also why the Christian faith makes the scandalous cross into the very center of meaning for human existence: it asserts that a suffering love which was not triumphant in history is nevertheless the light that shines in darkness, because faith apprehends this suffering love to be a revelation of the very nature of "ultimate reality."

Abraham Heschel, God in Search of Man

["Mysteries of Faith," *Saturday Review,* Vol. 39 (April 21, 1956), p. 18.]

ABRAHAM HESCHEL, who is a professor at the Jewish Theological Seminary in New York, has established himself as a creative interpreter of religious life and thought whose books have had an increasing hearing among both Jews and Christians. His former books, *The Earth Is the Lord's, The Sabbath,* which was a perceptive study of the Biblical view of time, and particularly his great volume *Man Is Not Alone,* reveal his rare gifts as poet, mystic, and interpreter of Biblical thought.

This new volume, *God in Search of Man,* enhances the gratitude of all readers who sense the authentically religious quality of his mind, in which Biblical thought is blended with the mystic quality of his Hasidic tradition in which he was nurtured. But the same volume is first of all an exposition of what Dr. Heschel terms the thought of "Biblical man." He shows what is unique in Biblical thought as distinct from classical mysticism, rationalism, and naturalism. Much of his volume is, therefore, not merely an exposition of the "philosophy of Judaism," but a treatise which will be found illuminating to all who regard Biblical thought as the source of one of the main streams of Western religious life.

Heschel is always conscious of the rational incomprehensibility of the divine mystery. He stands in the prophetic tradition with its warning: " 'My ways are not your ways and my thoughts not your thoughts,' saith the Lord." "Awe precedes faith and is at the root of faith," writes Heschel. "We must grow in awe in order to reach faith. Awe rather than faith is the cardinal attitude of the religious Jew." In Biblical language the religious man is not called a believer. "There is only one road to wisdom, which is awe." That is what is meant by the Biblical phrase

"The fear of the Lord is the beginning of wisdom." Thus Heschel sharply distinguishes the religious attitude from the scientific and philosophical attitudes which try to explain the world and to analyze its sequences.

The religious attitude is not only awe before mystery, but wonder before the "glory" of the divine. This glory is first of all the glory of the creator. Rationally we may analyze the world of nature, but religiously we sense the glory of creation behind and above the observed phenomena of the natural world.

But religious faith is more than awe before divine mystery; it is the reaction of trust to the disclosure of a specific meaning in the divine mystery. In the Bible, God is always hidden; but he is also revealed. Heschel has some eloquent words to say about the nature of "revelation" and the response of faith to revelation. His analysis of revelation will make it clear that historic religions do not merely cling to irrational theophanies which a better science and philosophy may dissolve. They are dealing with meanings which transcend the meanings ascertained by an analysis of the structures of the world. They see in some events (for the Jew the supreme event is the revelation on Mount Sinai) a revelatory power which gives meaning to the flux of events in history. Heschel devotes one of his most illuminating chapters to "The Paradox of Sinai."

It is, of course, at the point of revelation, when mystery is changed to specific meaning, that the skeptic who is not in the community of faith will ask his questions. He will ask the question, particularly, how arbitrariness is to be prevented in the ascertainment of the point of meaning. For in the disciplines of science and philosophy every effort is made to prevent arbitrariness by the test of coherence and correspondence to general experience. Heschel proves rather persuasively that all concepts of meaning which emerge from scientific and philosophical pursuits are inadequate for comprehending the mystery of human existence and of human history. But it is clear that religious trust ultimately depends upon a "leap of faith" which cannot be induced rationally. In a sense the whole volume is a defense of the Biblical thesis that "whosoever wishes to come to God must believe that He is." That is, the mystery transcending rational intelligibility must be assumed. It cannot be proved.

Heschel's volume is genuinely religious in that it seeks to give no rationally compelling arguments for religious faith, but rationally explicates the presuppositions and consequences of such a faith. Naturally, much of what he writes has equal relevance for Christians as well as Jews. But, in the nature of the case, the more specific the interpretations of the meaning of revelation become, the more he expounds the "philosophy of Judaism" rather than the general viewpoints of "Biblical man."

James MacGregor Burns, Roosevelt: The Lion and the Fox

["A Superb Portrait of FDR," *The New Leader,* Vol. 39 (December 10, 1956), pp. 11–12.]

BIOGRAPHY is, like portraiture, an art form. Professor Burns, a political scientist, has given us what the dust-jacket defines as the first "political biography." But the dust-jacket does not proclaim the chief merit of the book, which is that it is a work of art, in the sense that it gives us a clear portrait of the greatest political figure of the past generation. Roosevelt beguiled an isolationist nation from its isolationism and a conservative nation, dominated by the business creed of *laissez-faire,* to a pragmatic revolution. In that revolution, the whole nation came to accept the principle thesis of the "New Deal"—namely, that it is within the power and competence of the state to direct the political and economic life of a technical society for the purpose of assuring the general welfare and guaranteeing at least minimal securities to the people most exposed to the hazards of the complex machinery of a technical age.

In guiding the revolution, Roosevelt remade the Democratic party into an alliance of farmers, workers, racial minorities (including Negroes) and intellectuals—without excluding the Southern conservative wing of the party, which has been the solid core of its strength since the Civil War. Roosevelt did this job so well that we have just gone through a Presidential election in which a Republican President won a landslide victory, matching or surpassing those of Roosevelt, chiefly by the device of adopting the whole Roosevelt program in both domestic and foreign policy. Thus, the gains won in the Roosevelt era have been made secure through their unchallenged adoption by the opposition. One makes this judgment with some hesitancy in the present moment; there are indications that a general, who seemed absolutely committed to the idea of our responsibility as a hegemonous nation in the free world, may be embarking upon what has been defined as a "new isolationism," in which we go the "path of honor" alone, not being fully conscious of the perils to which our weaker allies are exposed.

Professor Burns is chiefly interested in the artistry by which Roosevelt beguiled very disparate political forces into the semblance of a unified program. He gives an illuminating account of the interaction between the leader of great political talent and the social forces which propel him into leadership and which are sometimes unwittingly loosed by the new direction which he has given public affairs. He does not pretend to give a full-scale account of Roosevelt's war leadership nor does he summarize, except in briefest terms, what we know from

Sherwood's *Roosevelt and Hopkins*. Perhaps because of this, Roosevelt emerges more the fox than the lion.

Burns recounts the years of apprenticeship of young Roosevelt as State Senator, anti-Tammany Wilsonian, Assistant Secretary of the Navy under Wilson, Vice Presidential candidate with Cox, and finally his triumph as Governor of New York, his struggle with Al Smith, and his careful plans for the Presidential nomination. One of the incidents in his rise to power described by Burns, which intrigued the present reader, is his dealing with the Jimmy Walker case in such a way as not to alienate Tammany too completely and yet preserve his reputation as an anti-Tammany Democrat. I was intrigued by the extreme dexterity with which Roosevelt allowed Walker to convict himself by the simple expedient of asking him to clarify point after point in the proceedings of the Seabury report, until Walker's guilt became quite clear. I marveled at the dexterity but questioned the political honesty of the Governor, who seemed to be assuring Walker that he assumed the Mayor's innocence, but what about this or that item of the voluminous Seabury report? My admiration for the fox in Roosevelt was not enough to persuade me to vote for him in 1932, but that is neither here nor there.

Burns's focus on Roosevelt's political artistry does not prevent him from giving a true portrait of the man himself, with his moods of gaiety and self-assurance; in the tragedy of his affliction from polio; in the touching relation with his wife, Eleanor, who literally drew him out of the depression consequent upon his illness by her absolute devotion and contended against his mother, who wanted her son to resign himself to the life of a country squire after his illness. Burns suggests that, despite the strong influence of that formidable matriarch upon Roosevelt's life, there never was a chance of Roosevelt renouncing his political ambitions. Burns also challenges the thesis that his "liberalism" was derived from his experiences during his illness. He was, after all, a rather enthusiastic Wilsonian long before that.

It is impossible to do justice to the many chapters of recent history which are illumined by the book: the early days of the New Deal: the fight over the "court-packing" scheme, in which Roosevelt lost many of his supporters and was in any case defeated; the third-term and fourth-term campaigns: his negotiations with Willkie, or rather the negotiations which never quite came off. Professor Burns suggests that these negotiations might have led to a creative new party alignment but that Roosevelt scared Willkie by his over-shrewd publicizing of the event in advance.

On the whole one gets what is, I think, a true impression of Roosevelt's skill as a political manipulator from Burns's account, together with the feeling that his skilled opportunism was frequently over-shrewd or even dishonest. In the light of subsequent charges by isolationists, it does not seem to me to be fair to accuse Roosevelt of not being honest with a nation which was caught in the toils of a neutralist mania and which did not recognize the international perils as clearly as Roosevelt saw them. If he had been less coy, the subsequent charges that he dragged us into the war would have been harder to refute. On the other hand, nothing but the passionate desire to win an election can quite explain, and certainly will not condone, the assurance which he gave the mothers in Boston that their sons would never fight in a foreign war. One must understand, of course, that the assurance was prompted by Willkie's sudden *volte-face* from being more interventionist than Roosevelt to the charge that Roosevelt was a "warmonger."

On the whole, Burns allows the record to unfold without too much judgment of the moral or political adequacy of the Rooseveltian policies. But he does allow himself some judgments which some of us will find rather unconvincing. "Roosevelt," he declares, for instance, "was in surprising degree a captive of the political forces around him, rather than their shaper." That judgment seems erroneous when one considers the achievement of remolding a rather moribund, Southern-based party into an instrument of Northern liberalism. On the other hand, Burns shows that Roosevelt did not consciously initiate the new dynamism of the labor movement, was rather ignorant of its importance, and only tardily came to the support of Senator Wagner in the passage of the Labor Relations Act. Since the rise of labor power is one of the most enduring consequences in the reshaping of the American economy and in the achievement of a more adequate equilibrium of social power in a technical age, this must be regarded as a curious irony of history.

Burns's analysis of Roosevelt's complex character as due to his "being a deeply divided man . . . lingering between two worlds" is rather unconvincing. The two worlds were, of course, the aristocratic world of Dutchess County, Groton, Harvard and "the right houses of Boston"; and the "world of Wilsonian reform at home and Wilsonian idealism abroad." That is surely not an adequate account of the complexity of his character. Churchill was more of an aristocrat than Roosevelt, and both men were enabled by their aristocratic tradition to have a certain freedom from the ethos of the business community, which both men challenged in their own way, Roosevelt in both domestic and foreign policy and Churchill in foreign policy (though he did fight for Lloyd George's revolutionary budget, which anticipated the New Deal by several decades). If there was a division in Roosevelt's soul, it must have been derived from the conflict between his ambition and will to power on the one hand and his "social idealism" on the other hand. But even this conflict could not have been too serious in a man who made the discovery that liberalism was a source of political power in the America of the Depression.

These minor criticisms are made merely to show that the reviewer has not lost all his critical faculties in his enjoyment of a superb work of art and an instructive account of the political and social history of a revolutionary and creative age, the temper of which will already seem strange to those who did not live through it and have grown into maturity in the modern complacency.

PART V
MISCELLANY

The Death of a Martyr

[*Christianity and Crisis,* Vol. 5 (June 25, 1945), pp. 6–7.] Dietrich Bonhoeffer was executed in a concentration camp shortly before the collapse of the Nazi regime. Soon afterward Niebuhr, who had known him and last seen him in Britain in 1939, wrote this reminiscence in which he paraphrased a letter, by then lost, which Bonhoeffer sent him a few months after that visit.

THE story of Bonhoeffer is worth recording. It belongs to the modern Acts of the Apostles. Bonhoeffer was one of the leaders of the Confessional Synod. He was the head of the secret theological seminary conducted by the Synod after the Nazis had corrupted the theological education of the universities. Despite his youth, for he was in his thirties, he was one of the most influential religious oppositional leaders in Germany. He was certainly the most uncompromising and heroic.

During the last two years Bonhoeffer was in and out of prison. He was in prison when the attempt was made on Hitler's life last June. He might have lost his own life at that time because he was an intimate adviser of some of the men who, inspired by religious motives participated in the plot on Hitler's life, hoping thereby to bring the evil Nazi regime to an end. He was actually sentenced to be executed; but his life was spared when the judge who sentenced him lost his life in a bomb raid upon Berlin before he had signed Bonhoeffer's death sentence. Delay in the certificate of execution first postponed and finally led to the commutation of the death sentence. It now appears, however, that the Nazis killed him and his brother Klaus, together with some known anti-Nazi leaders shortly before the American armies advanced upon his prison.

Bonhoeffer was a brilliant young theologian who combined a deep piety with a high degree of intellectual sophistication. He was strongly under the influence of Barthian theology. When he was in this country in 1930–31 as German fellow at Union Theological Seminary he was inclined to regard political questions as completely irrelevant to the life of faith. But as the Nazi evil rose he became more and more its uncompromising foe. With Barth he based his opposition to Nazism upon religious grounds. I still remember a discussion of theological and political matters I had with him in London in 1939 [ed. note: actually they met in a village of Sussex] when he assured me that Barth was right in becoming more political; but he criticized Barth for defining his position in a little pamphlet. "If" he declared in rather typical German fashion "one states an original position in many big volumes, one ought to define the change in one's position in an equally impressive volume and not in a little pamphlet." He himself was too busy in the affairs of a militant church to state his own position in many books. One book by him on "Discipleship" was written in 1937. But it is safe to say that his life and death will become one of the sources of grace for the new church in a new Germany.

In April of 1939 Bonhoeffer made one of his periodic visits to Britain, where he often conferred with ecumenical leaders, particularly with the Bishop of Chichester, who was then, as now, a kind of unofficial "protector" of Confessional Synod militants. At that time Bonhoeffer told me that Hitler would attack Poland before the end of the summer; that the executive committee of the Synod had agreed with him that he ought to leave Germany rather than be destroyed, since he was unalterably opposed to Hitler's war. It was felt that his life might well be saved for the work of the church after the war.

Quick communication to America procured for him the desired official invitations which were necessary to get him out of Germany. Dr. Coffin of Union Seminary arranged for various invitations, including one to teach in the summer school at the seminary.

The war had already begun when I next heard from him. He wrote somewhat to this effect: "Sitting here in Dr. Coffin's garden I have had the time to think and to pray about my situation and that of my nation and to have God's will for me clarified. I have come to the conclusion that I have made a mistake in coming to America. I must live through this difficult period of our national history with the Christian people of Germany. I will have no right to participate in the reconstruction of Christian life in Germany after the war if I do not share the trials of this time with my people. My brothers in the Confessional Synod wanted me to go. They may have been right in urging me to do so; but I was wrong in going. Such a decision each man must make for himself. Christians in Germany will face the terrible alternative of either willing the defeat of their nation in order that Christian civilization may survive, or willing the victory of their nation and thereby destroying our civilization. I know which of these alternatives I must choose; but I cannot make that choice in security."

Bonhoeffer had remarkably clear religious insights and the purity of a completely dedicated soul. Considering how recently he had developed his political and social interests, his shrewdness in assessing political and military tendencies was also remarkable. When Hitler invaded Russia and his armies stood deep in Russian territory, Bonhoeffer assured Dr. Visser t'Hooft, General Secretary of the World Council of Churches, that the Russian invasion spelt Hitler's doom. In 1942 he met his friend, the Bishop of Chichester, in Stockholm and gave him advance information on the *coup d'etat* involving an attempt on Hitler's life, which finally took place in June, 1944. He wanted the Bishop to let British and American authorities know that if certain people, whom he mentioned, were involved in the plot, they could regard it as a bona fide anti-Nazi venture. Unfortunately the little group which prepared this plot were in some respects too unskilled in the dangerous work which they undertook. Yet they came, according to reliable information, rather more closely to success than is usually assumed. But what the group lacked in skill it compensated for in devotion. Another young Christian layman, associated with Bonhoeffer, Adam von Tropp, was among the 19 who were executed.

Some American Christians have been rather dismayed by the fact that the great Martin Niemoeller, who has become the symbol of Protestant Christian resistance to Nazism, seems to have learned so little about the relation of Christian faith to civic virtue. The interviews he has given since his liberation prove the greatness of his soul but also his inability to transcend some of the errors which had dogged Christians in Germany, when dealing with matters of political justice and civic virtue. He still thinks that the church deals with men's souls and the state with their bodies, and thus he denies the spiritual unity of man in his various relationships.

Bonhoeffer, less known than Niemoeller, will become better known. Not only his martyr's death but also his actions and precepts contain within them the hope of a revitalized Protestant faith in Germany. It will be a faith, religiously more profound, than that of many of its critics; but it will have learned to overcome the one fateful error of German Protestantism, the complete dichotomy between faith and political life.

In an ecumenical group meeting in Geneva in 1941 Bonhoeffer made a remark which symbolizes the purity and the profundity of his faith. Asked for the content of his thought in a period of meditation he declared: "I am praying for the defeat of my nation. Only in and through defeat can it expiate the grievous wrong which it has done Europe and the world."

Modern Man and the Unknown Future

[*The Messenger,* Vol. 17 (January 15, 1952), p. 6.]

DR. MARTIN BUBER, the greatest living Jewish philosopher, has recently lectured in this country. Author of the book, *I and Thou*, which has influenced Christian theology as well as Jewish thought, he is an interpreter of the unique, dramatic, and personal nature of Biblical thought, as distinguished from the impersonal nature of scientific and philosophical thought.

The Bible is essentially the record of the dialogue of the soul with God and of the two subordinate dialogues of the soul with other souls and with itself. Life in the Bible is conceived as a series of dramatic encounters. The essence of real drama is derived from the "freedom" of the participants. For it is this freedom which makes for unpredictable future possibilities. We can predict the course of the stars. We can even predict the life course of a favorite domestic pet. Every animal runs through its life cycle, fulfilling its essential nature. But every child is unpredictable. We do not know what it may become or how it will work out its relations with others. The future of every human life is filled with unpredictable promises and perils.

If this is true of individual life, it is even more true of the whole human enterprise. All of us, like Abraham of old, go out, not knowing whither we go. The drama of human history is determined by God's providence and our decisions. These decisions are not as predictable as the course of nature because man is a genuinely responsible creature, who may succeed and may fail in any particular venture. Nothing has been more confusing to modern man than the effort of modern secular culture to reduce human history to the level of nature and to pretend that man was just about to achieve both knowledge and mastery of the future. This is impossible not only because human agents make unpredictable decisions in history but also because the Lord of history "taketh things that are not to put to naught the things that are." Thus both man's and God's freedom prevent human history from being simply predictable.

It is rather ironic that a civilization which thought it had reduced the human drama to predictable sequences should now confront a world situation in which our future is more unknown than at any time in recent centuries. When we fought the Nazis, we did not know the exact outcome but we had a considerable certainty that Nazism was a form of evil which would destroy itself.

Now Communism is another great evil. But it may attract millions of people in Asia before it finally disintegrates. We have to do what we can to prevent its spread, but no one can give us any certainty about the consequences of our acts.

The tendency in some circles of America to wish for a "preventive" war may have many roots, but surely a primary root is the impious desire to control the future or rather the impious impatience with an uncertain future. It is an ironic judgment upon modern man—who thought he knew so much—that he must learn to live by faith rather than by sight as he walks into the future; and must be content to know that "sufficient unto the day is the evil thereof."

The Abundance of Things a Man Possesses

[*The Messenger,* Vol. 20 (August 16, 1955), p. 7.]

IT is a scriptural maxim "a man's life does not consist in the abundance of his possessions." The Scriptures also warn us: "What will it profit a man, if he gains the whole world and forfeits his life?" This warning assumes that there is some contradiction between the things of the world and the integrity or serenity of the soul.

We are in grave danger in America of violating the spiritual principles on which these warnings are based. It is not that the Christian faith glorifies poverty as an end in itself or despises the body and the body's health. The comparative well-being of the people of Western civilization in contrast to the poverty of the Orient is due to the life-affirming and history-affirming character of the Christian faith. The late Archbishop of Canterbury, Dr. William Temple, rightly defined Christianity as the most "materialistic" of religions. It emphasizes that the soul and the body are a unity and that redemption is something else than the emancipation of the soul from the body.

Nevertheless, the same faith warns against being overwhelmed by the "cares of this world." The question is whether the preoccupation of the American culture with the comforts of this life, with ever higher standards of living, with automobiles and refrigerators, vacuum cleaners and television, and all the other gadgets of the "American way of life"—whether this is not a real peril to our soul.

Only two decades ago we were in a depression, and everyone looked toward the redemptive possibilities of an "economy of abundance." Now we have such an economy. The total national product of goods and services has gone far beyond the three hundred billion mark. We enjoy a standard of living beyond the dreams of avarice of the rest of the world. That is also one of the reasons for our unpopularity in the poorer nations of the world, where envy no doubt colors judgment somewhat.

The greater portion of our wealth is due to the remarkable efficiency of our technics, to our industrial enterprise, and to the ingenuity of our applied sciences. But it cannot be denied that such wealth could not have been accumulated without straining after the comforts of life. The world regards this preoccupation of our culture as "vulgar," and we shall no doubt find, in due time, that the comforts of life are subject to a law of diminishing returns in assuring us true happiness.

Such happiness ultimately transcends the comforts of life and depends upon a serenity and integrity of soul which are not at all related to standards of living. Let the preacher beware who has just traded his old car for a new and better one, lest his exposition of scriptural faith be belied by his actions! It is very difficult to draw the line between a rightful and a sinful preoccupation with life's comforts.

This problem is undoubtedly one of the chief spiritual issues confronting our nation. It can neither be solved by mere strictures against riches nor by a glorification of creature comforts. The question is where each of us will draw the line. It is perhaps the most important question for every exponent and beneficiary of the "American way of life."

For Our Inheritance: A Thanksgiving Prayer

[*Prayers for Services: A Manual for Leaders of Worship,* compiled and edited by Morgan Phelps Noyes (New York: Charles Scribner's Sons, 1945), pp. 80–81.]

WE thank thee, our Father, for life and love, for the mystery and majesty of existence, for the world of beauty which surrounds us and for the miracle of our conscious life by which we behold the wonders of the universe.

We thank thee for the glimpses of nobility in human life which redeem it from sordidness and reassure us that thy image is in the heart of man. We are grateful for the ties which bind us to our fellow men; for our common toil in industry and marts of trade; for our joint inheritance as citizens of this nation; for traditions and customs hallowed by age through which our passions are ordered and channeled; for the love of beauty and truth and goodness by which we transcend the chasms of race and nation; for the faith of our fathers by which we claim kinship with the past and gain strength for the present; for the love of dear ones in our homes and for the enlarging responsibilities and sobering duties of family life; for the serenity of old people who redeem us from fretfulness; and for the faith and courage of youth through which we are saved from sloth.

We are not worthy of the rich inheritances of our common life. We confess that we have profaned the temple of this life by our selfishness and heedlessness. We have sought to gain advantage of our brothers who are bound to us by many different ties. Have mercy upon us, that we may express our gratitude for thy many mercies by contrition for our sins and that we may prove our repentance by lives dedicated more fully to thee and to the common good; through Jesus Christ our Lord. Amen.